POP CULTURE LEGENDS

BOB DYLAN

★ ★

SUSAN RICHARDSON

CHELSEA HOUSE PUBLISHERS

New York ★ Philadelphia

BOB DYLAN

★ ★ ★ ★ ★ ★ ★ ★ ★ ★ ★ ★ ★ ★

CHELSEA HOUSE PUBLISHERS

EDITORIAL DIRECTOR   Richard Rennert
EXECUTIVE MANAGING EDITOR   Karyn Gullen Browne
COPY CHIEF   Robin James
PICTURE EDITOR   Adrian G. Allen
CREATIVE DIRECTOR   Robert Mitchell
ART DIRECTOR   Joan Ferrigno
PRODUCTION MANAGER   Sallye Scott

Pop Culture Legends
SENIOR EDITOR   Kathy Kuhtz Campbell
SERIES DESIGN   Basia Niemczyc

Staff for BOB DYLAN
EDITORIAL ASSISTANT   Scott D. Briggs
PICTURE RESEARCHER   Ellen Barrett Dudley
COVER ILLUSTRATION   Jon Weiman

First Printing

1 3 5 7 9 8 6 4 2

Library of Congress Cataloging-in-Publication Data

Richardson, Susan.
Bob Dylan/Susan Richardson.
p. cm.—(Pop culture legends)
Includes bibliographical references and index.
ISBN 0-7910-2335-4
1. Dylan, Bob, 1941–. 2. Singers—United States—Biography. [1. Dylan, Bob, 1941–. 2. Musicians.] I. Title. II. Series.
ML3930.D97R53 1994   94-35617
782.42162'0092—dc20   CIP
[B]   AC MN

Contents ★ ★ ★ ★ ★ ★ ★ ★ ★ ★ ★ ★ ★ ★ ★ ★ ★ ★ ★

A Reflection of Ourselves

Leeza Gibbons

I ENJOY A RARE PERSPECTIVE on the entertainment industry. From my window on popular culture, I can see all that sizzles and excites. I have interviewed legends who have left us, such as Bette Davis and Sammy Davis, Jr., and have brushed shoulders with the names who have caused a commotion with their sheer outrageousness, like Boy George and Madonna. Whether it's by nature or by design, pop icons generate interest, and I think they are a mirror of who we are at any given time.

Who are *your* heroes and heroines, the people you most admire? Outside of your own family and friends, to whom do you look for inspiration and guidance, as examples of the type of person you would like to be as an adult? How do we decide who will be the most popular and influential members of our society?

You may be surprised by your answers. According to recent polls, you will probably respond much differently than your parents or grandparents did to the same questions at the same age. Increasingly, world leaders such as Winston Churchill, John F. Kennedy, Franklin D. Roosevelt, and evangelist Billy Graham have been replaced by entertainers, athletes, and popular artists as the individuals whom young people most respect and admire. In surveys taken during each of the past 15 years, for example, General Norman Schwarzkopf was the only world leader chosen as the number-one hero among high school students. Other names on the elite list joined by General Schwarzkopf included Paula Abdul, Michael Jackson, Michael Jordan, Eddie Murphy, Burt Reynolds, and Sylvester Stallone.

More than 30 years have passed since Canadian sociologist Marshall McLuhan first taught us the huge impact that the electronic media have had on how we think, learn, and understand—as well as how we choose our heroes. In the 1960s, Pop artist Andy Warhol predicted that there would soon come a time when every American would be famous for 15 minutes. But if it is easier today to achieve Warhol's 15 minutes of fame, it is also much harder to hold on to it. Reputations are often ruined as quickly as they are made.

And yet, there remain those artists and performers who continue to inspire and instruct us in spite of changes in world events, media technology, or popular tastes. Even in a society as fickle and fast moving as our own, there are still those performers whose work and reputation endure, pop culture legends who inspire an almost religious devotion from their fans.

Why do the works and personalities of some artists continue to fascinate us while others are so quickly forgotten? What, if any, qualities do they share that enable them to have such power over our lives? There are no easy answers to these questions. The artists and entertainers profiled in this series often have little more in common than the enormous influence that each of them has had on our lives.

Some offer us an escape. Artists such as actress Marilyn Monroe, comedian Groucho Marx, and writer Stephen King have used glamour, humor, or fantasy to help us escape from our everyday lives. Others present us with images that are all too recognizable. The uncompromising realism of actor and director Charlie Chaplin and folk singer Bob Dylan challenges us to confront and change the things in our world that most disturb us.

Some offer us friendly, reassuring experiences. The work of animator Walt Disney and late-night talk show host Johnny Carson, for example, provides us with a sense of security and continuity in a changing world. Others shake us up. The best work of composer John Lennon and actor James Dean will always inspire their fans to question and reevaluate the world in which they live.

It is also hard to predict the kind of life that a pop culture legend will lead, or how he or she will react to fame. Popular singers Michael Jackson

and Prince carefully guard their personal lives from public view. Other performers, such as popular singer Madonna, enjoy putting their private lives before the public eye.

What these artists and entertainers do share, however, is the rare ability to capture and hold the public's imagination in a world dominated by mass media and disposable celebrity. In spite of their differences, each of them has somehow managed to achieve legendary status in a popular culture that values novelty and change.

The books in this series examine the lives and careers of these and other pop culture legends, and the society that places such great value on their work. Each book considers the extraordinary talent, the stubborn commitment, and the great personal sacrifice required to create work of enduring quality and influence in today's world.

As you read these books, ask yourself the following questions: How are the careers of these individuals shaped by their society? What role do they play in shaping the world? And what is it that so captivates us about their lives, their work, or the images they present?

Hopefully, by studying the lives and achievements of these pop culture legends, we will learn more about ourselves.

Thirty Years and Counting

ON THE MELLOW AUTUMN EVENING of October 16, 1992, as New York City shifted from its workday gear into its nighttime one, traffic was thicker than usual around Madison Square Garden. The massive indoor arena, which houses major events from basketball games to rock concerts, had even been the site of the Democratic National Convention some three months earlier. On this particular night in October, however, the Garden would be the scene of one of the most remarkable tributes in rock music's history. Singer and songwriter Bob Dylan had turned 50 the year before and was celebrating the 30th anniversary of his first album, *Bob Dylan*. But, more than these two single events, the unusual concert to be held that night would formally commemorate the career of a man whose work had profoundly shaped the course of popular music.

Fans filled the arena. The Garden was frequently packed for concerts, but what made this evening different from others was the price of tickets for the event. The company for whom Dylan recorded, Columbia Records, spon-

At his 30th anniversary tribute on October 16, 1992, Bob Dylan chose to sing two songs from early in his career: "Song to Woody," his 1962 homage to the "Dust Bowl Balladeer" Woody Guthrie, and "It's Alright, Ma (I'm Only Bleeding)," his 1965 masterful message of protest.

11

sored the concert, and the official ticket price had run as high as $80 per seat. Tickets that had been scalped, or resold illegally, had cost even more. The concert was sold out almost as soon as the tickets went on sale. Press passes, usually free for the upper echelons of the music business, were few, expensive, and hard to come by. In other words, those who attended the concert that night had worked hard to get there.

The crowd was restless and diverse. It was well known that the concert would be a "Dylanfest," and that many popular rock-and-roll artists of both older and younger generations would honor Bob Dylan by performing songs that he had written over the course of his 30-year career. However, exactly who would sing, and what and when, remained unclear. The feeling of anticipation pervaded the Garden; but there was an aura of edginess, too, as the still-empty stage punctuated the unpredictability of what was to come.

Finally, the spotlights illuminated the stage. John Cougar Mellencamp, a rock-and-roll singer from Indiana, and his band members and backup singers walked on and took their places. The crowd lit up like spreading fire as Mellencamp waved his hands high in the air. Mellencamp's drummer, Kenny Aranoff, cracked his drumsticks together and jump-started the band—and, with it, the arena—into a burning version of one of Dylan's most powerful and renowned songs, "Like a Rolling Stone." Dylan's celebration was underway.

It was somehow appropriate that such a monolithic fete honoring Dylan, who had been seen as the poetic and political figurehead of a generation, would fall in the midst of New York City and the political apprehension of the 1992 presidential election year. The city and the anxiety were, in a way, mutual mirrors, emblematic of the excesses of the 1980s and the highs and lows that had emerged from the previous 12 years. Wealth was juxtaposed with destitution, high-level financiers with communities ravaged by AIDS, drugs, and gangs. Homeless people sought refuge in every area of the city. Immigration from other countries had reached a record high, and people from diverse cultures, with different religions and languages, struggled to find ways to both coexist and retain their distinctiveness without resorting to discrimination. After the Republican party's domination of national politics under President Ronald Reagan and then President George Bush, the Democratic party was attempting to bring these social issues under some control. For the first time since the 1970s, there was a widespread belief that social concerns should not be peripheral in national politics, but central. For many young people, the decade of the 1990s was the first one that they could recall there being a sense of social focus at all.

Into this social and political context fell the concert for Dylan who, since the beginning of his career in 1960, has been seen as a poet, a political activist, a consummate musician, a wanderer, and a mystery. His music draws on almost every stream of American music, including rock and roll, blues, gospel, folk, and country. His lyrics span a poetic gamut that has brought rage, poignancy, irony, flippancy, and political passion within the realm of popular music. His life has been one of exploration. And even when Dylan fails to live up to the prophetic vision often ascribed to him by his fans, he is perhaps all the more honest for his curiosity, vulnerability, and unfiltered expressiveness, for his ability to be touched.

Furthermore, it is the range of people that Dylan, in turn, has touched that gave the concert its impetus. Artists from all areas of popular music, from Dylan's own generation of 1960s rockers to today's youngest pathfinders, converged on the stage that night and found voice—pathos, urgency, and contemporary relevance—in his songs.

Stevie Wonder entered, sat down at the keyboard, and, over an indeterminate vamp, began to talk about the song he was about to sing. He did not give its name but rather talked about its history. He mentioned the song's applicability to the civil rights movement during the 1960s, when African Americans across the country struggled for social equality, as well as its relation to the war in Vietnam, to the Watergate scandal of the 1970s, and to Stephen Biko, the martyr of the struggle against South African apartheid. Wonder went on to refer to the pending presidential election and asked the audience to vote for whomever "commits to bringing unity to all people." When he sang the song — "Blowin' in the Wind," which the folk group Peter, Paul and Mary had made a popular hit some 25 years before—the audience cheered. Wonder's version was typically ornate and wrought with deep empathy. For all its history, the song made a fresh, clear, and direct statement, which, based on the crowd's response, hit its mark.

Lou Reed, a solo artist formerly of the Velvet Underground, sang "Foot of Pride," which Dylan had written in 1983 during his time as a disciple of Christianity. The song, over spare instrumentals and driving rhythm, elaborates moralistically on the idea that "pride goeth before a fall." Reed gave it a heavier groove that had more gravity in every backbeat. An artist who, in his own songs (such as "Busload of Faith"), had coaxed hope out of cynicism, Reed remarkably embraced the sensibility of the original song, expanding its moral weight as well as its innocent tone. Eddie Vedder and Mike McCready, from the new and influential group Pearl Jam, performed "Masters of War," finding in it the rich potential for young people to plead for compassion in the wake of wealth and materialism. Folk music heroine Tracy Chapman sang "The Times They Are A-Changin'." Country-music legends Johnny Cash and June Carter Cash sang

"It Ain't Me, Babe," and Willie Nelson gave a country-flavored rendition of "What Was It You Wanted."

When Sinead O'Connor, an Irish singer and political activist, took the stage, her presence evoked assorted reactions from the audience. Only a few weeks earlier, in a highly publicized appearance on the television show "Saturday Night Live," she had torn up a picture of Pope John Paul II to protest what she saw as social oppression by the Roman Catholic church. Her gesture sparked much controversy, and the artist found herself the focus of widespread criticism. That night, at Madison Square Garden, the audience epitomized that controversy, roaring back an indiscernible and unanticipated mix of emotions. The keyboardist, Booker T, played the opening bars to the song "I Believe in You," which O'Connor had planned to sing, but she motioned him silent. He stopped. The crowd roared on. Kris Kristofferson, who was hosting the concert, walked over and said to O'Connor, "Don't let the bastards get you down."

Many friends and colleagues joined Dylan (center) at his celebration at New York's Madison Square Garden, including (from left to right) Eric Clapton, George Harrison, Roger McGuinn (with back to camera), George Thorogood, Tom Petty, and Carolyn Hester.

"I'm not down," she replied. But her demeanor had darkened. She grasped the microphone, brought it close to her face, and, with no accompaniment, yelled the first verse of a completely different song, not one by Dylan at all. It was a reggae protest song called "War," by Bob Marley. She finished and walked quickly offstage, while the audience continued its clatter. The audience's reaction to O'Connor, as well as hers to it, had been unplanned, disruptive, and disconcerting. However, in that the exchange was a spontaneous and controversial expression of social concerns, it was not wholly inappropriate at a celebration of Dylan's legacy. Stagehands scrambled to prepare for the next performer, and shortly thereafter momentum was restored, as Neil Young appeared and began to sing "Just Like Tom Thumb's Blues."

The parade of artists continued and included Eric Clapton, Roger McGuinn of the Byrds, Tom Petty and the Heartbreakers, and George Harrison. The rhythm-and-blues group the O'Jays sang "Emotionally Yours," a song from 1985. They had previously taken it to the top of the rhythm-and-blues charts, and their performance that night turned the love song into fervent, cohesive, and expansive gospel. The Band, the group who had played backup for Dylan during the mid-1960s and had become successful in their own right, paid tribute with a rich rendition of a lesser-known Dylan song, "When I Paint My Masterpiece."

Finally, after an introduction by George Harrison, Bob Dylan walked onstage. In the wake of such revelry, it would have seemed natural for Dylan to enter with flair or grandiosity, bringing to a climax the audience's long evening of anticipation. But he did not. Rather than showing celebrity, self-acknowledgment, or, for that matter, self-enjoyment, he seemed like a bystander, incidental to the flow of the evening. He did little to recognize the exuberant crowd but only positioned his harmonica and guitar and moved up to the microphone. What he chose to sing was even more curious. He bypassed the greatest hits, the popular favorites, and turned instead to two quiet songs from early in his career.

The first was "Song to Woody" and, appropriately, had been on his first album. He had written it to honor singer Woody Guthrie (1912–67), the folk hero who had remained a compelling figure for Dylan throughout his life. The lyrics speak of traveling in a difficult and torn world and refer to musicians, like Guthrie, who have been absorbed into a vague musical past. The final two verses, in particular, lead to a place of loneliness and transience, as they allude to old folk-blues singers Cisco Houston and Leadbelly, who had traveled and performed with, and inspired, Guthrie.

Like Guthrie, their music had sprung from the reality of the difficulties of life during the 1930s, and they, like Guthrie, wholly experienced that life until the inevitable ending—death. It was almost as if Dylan were insisting that the audience leave behind any illusory hope, evoked even for a moment by such an event, of immortality, ease, or resolution. In the lyrics of the song he chose, everyone in Madison Square Garden—on- and offstage—was placed on the same transitory plateau.

The other song Dylan sang was "It's Alright, Ma (I'm Only Bleeding)," about the attempt to achieve integrity in the midst of social corruption. But the song goes far beyond mere cynicism over political dishonesty. It becomes, instead, a wrenching statement about the tenuous search for "self" and the destruction that results when one fails to find it. Dylan's lyrics roam through places of confusion, caught between the voices in the world around him telling him who he is or how he should act, and his own instinct, which recognizes that those images do not ring true—yet in the end, he has no alternatives. The singer brings himself to the desolate statement, beyond

During the grand finale of the "Dylanfest," the performers collaborated with the guest of honor in singing "My Back Pages" (1964) and "Knockin' on Heaven's Door" (1973).

criticism or irony, that there is simply nothing left to look to.

The lyrics were appropriate for the confused and highly charged politics of the election year. Yet it seemed, again, that Dylan was speaking of an even more personal experience. There was no sense of moral victory in the song, only a feeling of continued search and struggle. The 30th anniversary of a career had been achieved—and ritualized—but nothing had been resolved.

Beyond the choices of these two songs, Dylan's performance style itself lent the final ironic touch to the figure who was the focus of such a massive media event. He slouched, his movements were inhibited, and he seemed reluctant to become the center of attention. His voice had always been ragged and dark, but now it was even less comforting—flat, two-dimensional, and nasal. His singing was almost indecipherable, and it seemed as though, once again, he had refused to play the role of a public idol.

For the evening's two grand finales, the musicians all reappeared to join Dylan in renditions of "My Back Pages" and "Knockin' on Heaven's Door." During these songs, Dylan ducked aimlessly behind the other performers, almost willfully losing himself in the crowd. After the renditions, the momentum of the evening gradually dissipated. Those onstage began to mingle and talk among themselves. Some improvised music. Friendly and informal, it was a rare moment for such a revered mix of artists.

That night, the Dylan tribute brought together representatives of nearly every type of popular music, politics, personal style, and commitment from three decades of rock in a way that no one could have purposely designed. From Stevie Wonder to Sinead O'Connor to the Band, the concert truly illustrated the expressive, germane, and highly diverse forum that rock and roll had become. As the evening made clear, at the heart of rock's history, within the strands that united this diversity, lay the powerful songs of a man from Minnesota, whose career had shaped so many aspects of rock's unfolding.

At their conception, Dylan's songs of protest had heralded change. Today they still retain a striking resonance, evoking old social concerns and moral issues while accommodating the new. But beyond that realm, Dylan's songs continue to capture in a satisfying and compelling way a range of personal experiences—experiences that include political conviction but lie beyond it as well. It is this ability to probe and articulate such a variety of feelings that distinguishes Dylan's work from others'. Together his songs create a map of human emotions, outlining and exploring the places where people find themselves feeling alone, wonderful, strange, or frightened. Dylan never offers an easy way out of these places, or a way to avoid reentry. Instead, over the years, his songs have simply acknowledged that the places do exist, and that it is all right to be there.

2 Zimmerman to Dylan

BOB DYLAN only became Bob Dylan when he was a young adult. He was born Robert Allen Zimmerman on May 24, 1941, in Duluth, Minnesota. His grandfather, Zigman Zimmerman, was a Jew who had left the Ukrainian city of Odessa in 1907 to escape the anti-Semitism of Czarist Russia. Zigman immigrated to the United States and settled in Duluth. Throughout his life, Dylan remained aware of the legacy of the persecution of Jews in Russia and elsewhere in Europe, especially during World War II, and some of his songs would allude to discrimination in general, as well as to the specific experience of the Jewish people.

Dylan's parents, Beatrice "Beattie" Stone and Abraham "Abe" Zimmerman, met at a New Year's Eve party in Duluth in 1932. Beattie was from the small town of Hibbing, Minnesota, near the Canadian border, and had driven her father's car to the big city of Duluth, alone, in search of a New Year's celebration. Abe Zimmerman admired her confidence and wit, and Beattie liked the fact that Abe had a steady job at the Standard Oil Company. The couple married two years later. In the late spring of 1941, as World War II

At a November 1962 Columbia Records session in New York, Dylan sings one of his songs for *The Freewheelin' Bob Dylan* album. Years later, Dylan said, "New York was a dream. . . . It was a dream of cosmopolitan riches of the mind. It was the greatest place for me to learn and to meet other people who were on similar journeys."

21

was raging in Europe, the Zimmermans gave birth to their first child, a boy with thick blond hair, named Robert Allen. Their second son, David, was born in February 1946.

In 1947, Dylan's parents moved from Duluth to Hibbing. Hibbing, like many other small towns, felt the optimism, prosperity, and conformism (that is, conformity to a conservative, mainstream image) that had followed World War II. Somewhat geographically isolated from the pressing concerns of most urban centers in postwar America, Hibbing became more directly touched by national events with the onset of radio, movies, and television. By the mid-1950s, it, too, felt the social tensions that were rolling across the country. Senator Joseph McCarthy of Wisconsin, under the aegis of a special congressional subcommittee during the early 1950s, sought out people whom he felt might hold radical political convictions, specifically those sympathetic to communism. He summoned them before the subcommittee, cross-examined them, hectored them, and accused mostly innocent citizens of being Communists and of posing a threat to American democracy. This political practice of publicizing accusations of alleged subversion without regard to evidence became known as McCarthyism, and it encouraged a conservative trend in national politics and a suspicion of left-wing views.

Meanwhile, the civil rights movement, the struggle for social equality for blacks as well as for whites, was gaining momentum. In 1954, the U.S. Supreme Court, in the case of *Brown vs. Board of Education of Topeka,* declared that segregation of the races in public schools violated the equal protection clause of the Fourteenth Amendment of the U.S. Constitution, and that the "separate but equal" doctrine, which had been in effect since the late 19th century, was no longer valid. The Supreme Court's deci-

sion launched the long, violent struggle against prejudice nationwide, but most fervently in the South.

While this social revolution was being fought, Elvis Presley, Chuck Berry, and Little Richard played what became known as rock-and-roll music, music that gave teenagers their own mode of expression and an identity that was distinct from that of adults. The early rock-and-roll singers also gave voice to the rhythm and blues of African Americans and the country music of poor southerners, who had felt ignored by the white middle class in society. And in film, movie actors like James Dean, Marlon Brando, and Montgomery Clift profoundly impressed upon a generation of young men the idea of the self-determined rebel, a characterization that seemed to coincide with the defiant style of rock-and-roll music. All of these elements—conformism, social revolution, rock-and-roll music, and the unconventional movie hero—converged to create for the young Dylan, as for many others, a perception of mainstream America and of the rebel beyond it.

Seen here in 1948, Howard Street, the main thoroughfare of Hibbing, Minnesota, consisted of a movie theater, cafés, auto supply stores, and gas stations. The Zimmermans—Abe, Beattie, Bob, and David—moved from Duluth to the small town of Hibbing in 1947.

As a child, Dylan was comfortable being the center of attention and on occasion would reportedly sing for the people who worked in his father's office at Standard Oil. Just before his fifth birthday, he sang for the guests gathered for a Mother's Day party at the Zimmerman home. His mother later described that performance: "He stamped his foot and commanded attention. Bobby said, 'If everyone in this room will keep quiet, I will sing for my grandmother. I'm going to sing 'Some Sunday Morning.' Well, he sang it, and they tore the place apart. They clapped so hard that he sang his other big number, 'Accentuate the Positive.' He didn't know much more than those two songs."

As early as age 10 or 11, Dylan began to write poems. Just as with his early vocal performances, Mother's Day provided an occasion for creativity. One year, he wrote to his mother:

> My dear mother, I hope that you
> Will never grow old and gray,
> So that all the people in the world will say:
> "Hello, young lady, Happy Mother's Day."

Although Dylan had no formal music lessons, he nevertheless began to compose musically as well, pounding on the piano. Around the age of 14, he took up the guitar and shortly thereafter formed a band called the Golden Chords. In the band, Dylan played rhythm guitar—strumming along rhythmically on the prominent chords in a song—while another friend played lead guitar, taking solos and melodies, and a third, the drums. The Golden Chords played frequently at school assemblies, dances, and restaurants. Though the audience's reaction to his performances was often mixed, Dylan nonetheless plunged ahead, pleased with his own exploratory music-making. He went on to play with one or two other rock bands during high school, including Elston

Gunn & His Rock Boppers. One of his fellow guitar players later related that "It wasn't a matter of trying to be a group. It was Bob being pretty much of a personality. He was Little Richard, with rhythm in the background. This was strictly Little Richard."

Even during these early efforts, Dylan felt the influence of the different musical streams that were flowing in the United States, such as the country style of Hank Williams, folk music, and the blues. But it was to early rock and roll that the young Dylan particularly responded: the emerging rockabilly performed by Elvis Presley and Jerry Lee Lewis, as well as Little Richard's exuberant, sexual rock. The stated goal beside Dylan's picture in the 1959 Hibbing High School yearbook was "To join Little Richard." And a few years later, the first single he planned to record for Columbia Records was "Mixed Up Confusion," a song in the rockabilly style.

Dylan made no known recordings until after he was 18 years old. As a teenager, he spent much time writing his own music and lyrics, and it was during this period that he established his basic identity as a singer who accompanied himself on the guitar. He also experimented with the different melodies and timbres, or sound qualities, that the guitar could make. The experimentations were not always subtle. Around 1958, Dylan's band performed at Hibbing High School's Jacket Jamboree Talent Festival. Dylan turned up the amplifiers as loud as they could possibly go, to the surprise of the audience and the chagrin of the principal. Even at this time, Dylan was pushing beyond what was considered to be acceptable boundaries.

In the summer of 1959, after graduating from Hibbing High School, Dylan struck out on his own, working as a busboy at the Red Apple Café in Fargo, North Dakota, where he occasionally played the piano in singer Bobby Vee's band. But more important, he began to pay increasing attention to folksingers, such as Judy Collins and Jesse Fuller, whom he met around 1960. Collins, Fuller, and others like them were rapidly gaining popularity as musicians who wrote and performed songs that were relevant to social issues, particularly the civil rights movement, the struggle for social equality that was gaining momentum in the early 1960s. Dylan was drawn into

Little Richard, whose song "Tutti Frutti" became a hit in 1955, performs at Toronto's Maple Leaf Gardens in July 1956. As a teenager, Bob idolized the pulsating music of Little Richard, and in his high school yearbook he gave as his goal: "To join Little Richard."

both the musical style and the social message of this movement.

In the fall of 1959 he headed for the University of Minnesota, in Minneapolis. Dylan was immediately attracted to a district in Minneapolis called Dinkytown, a bohemian neighborhood where many poets, musicians, and artists lived and performed. After his first semester at the University of Minnesota, he spent very little time in class, concentrating instead on his music. He sang wherever he could, frequently ending up at a Minneapolis café called the Ten O'Clock Scholar or at the Purple Onion pizza parlor in the neighboring city of St. Paul.

Dylan's performance style sometimes drew applause and sometimes criticism from his audiences. He sang with a nasal tone and did not always pronounce the words to the songs clearly, which some audiences did not like, but which would become his trademark sound. It was also during this time that he began to perform with a harmonica and a guitar. He would strap a harmonica holder over the top of his shoulders, positioning the harmonica up in front of his mouth so that he could play both instruments simultaneously. He played the guitar in an uncomplicated, basic way, with no interest in flashy or smooth technique. But this combination of a rough voice and simple guitar accompaniment, punctuated by the harmonica's phrases, soon became integral to his identity. This early in his growth, Dylan was able to weave these different sounds into a single texture that was both unpretentious and highly expressive.

It was during his performing days in Dinkytown that the young Bob Zimmerman first began using the name "Bob Dylan" as his stage name. The singer has never been clear about the reasons he adopted Dylan as a surname. The Welsh poet Dylan Thomas may have provided the most likely inspiration. Widespread interest in Thomas's poetry had followed his death in 1953, and Dylan's awareness of Thomas's work coincided with the young singer's confrontation of his own poetic identity. However, Bob Dylan himself denies any association with Dylan Thomas, claiming instead that the surname was a whimsical choice. Whatever its source, the name gave him a public image distinct from his Jewish midwestern roots and a historical resonance that could only enhance the young Dylan's career.

But beyond his experimentation with music and image, a far more influential factor emerged from Dylan's Minneapolis experience. While there, he became profoundly influenced by a figure who quickly emerged as one of the most powerful in his life: folksinger and social activist Woody Guthrie. When Dylan had first heard of him, Guthrie was already suffering from Huntington's chorea in a hospital in New Jersey. (Huntington's chorea is a rare, hereditary disease of the nervous system that results in the rapid onset of jerky, involuntary movements; slow, agonizing mental deterioration; and eventually, death.) Guthrie would die of the disease in October 1967. But during the late 1950s, his music, politics, and personal style had a huge effect on Dylan and many other young people who became involved in both the folkmusic revival, spearheaded by such artists as Pete Seeger and the Almanac Singers, the Weavers, and the Kingston Trio, and the civil rights movement. Traveling throughout the United States during the Great Depression, the drought of 1935, and the union rallies of the late 1930s, Guthrie was a firsthand witness to widespread and devastating social ills, such as poverty and its moral counterparts, greed and waste. Guthrie wrote about these experiences both in his autobiography, *Bound for Glory* (1943), which Dylan hungrily consumed, and in his songs, with compassion, conviction, and icy irony. Guthrie wrote some 1,000 songs, including "This Land Is Your Land," "Pastures of Plenty," and

"Union Maid," and he was vocal about his desire for the songs to be part of social action. That ideal stayed with Dylan, as did Guthrie's performance style: a rough, haggard voice with guitar accompaniment in a folk-music idiom. Many of his songs were anthemlike and inspired Dylan's songs of protest, including "The Times They Are A-Changin'." Guthrie's song lyrics were simple and aphoristic, and his political vision and conviction, articulated in his music, reverberated throughout America.

By the end of 1960, Bob Zimmerman had truly become Bob Dylan as he undertook the biggest move of his life. Wanting to "make it in New York" and to meet Guthrie personally, he traveled in 1961 to New York City. As he had done in Minneapolis, he immediately gravitated toward the bohemian area of New York, Greenwich Village, where he made the rounds of the cafés and other establishments in which the folk artists and other musicians congregated. In addition to the artistic exploration that went on among the musicians who spent most of their time in the Village, there was an atmosphere of social compassion and hope, a hope that was personified in the figure of John F. Kennedy, the newly elected president of the United States. A belief in the ability of art and music to have an effect on the social conscience of the people around them aroused a particular conviction among these artists and inspired their songs and poems.

Dylan's friends and fellow musicians who knew him well during the early 1960s were struck by one characteristic above all others: he could hear a song once and learn it by heart. Dylan seemed to be a sponge, "blotting paper," according to folksinger Liam Clancy. Clancy added that Dylan "had this immense curiosity; he was totally blank, and ready to suck up everything that came within his range." From country to blues to various folk traditions, Dylan studied other musicians so closely that it appeared as though he learned by osmosis.

Despite his early interest in rock, Dylan's music during these days came to be folk oriented. The late 1950s and early 1960s were lean years for rock and roll. Much of the verve that Presley and Little Richard had brought to rock and roll had faded, and popular music had become less controversial and more fragmented. But folk music, associated as it was with more radical politics and social issues, seemed livelier, more substantial, and more unified—all attractive ingredients to an aspiring political songwriter. Dylan began his New York career by singing older songs that had been part of an oral folk tradition—passed down from performer to performer for many generations. During the folk-music revival that Dylan saw going on around him, many people believed that the various folk traditions, such as English, Scottish, or Appalachian, were mutually exclusive. In other words, to be truly pure, a singer should perform the music of one heritage as it had always been sung. However, Dylan eschewed this idea, singing what he liked and varying it as he pleased. It was during this time that he traveled out to Greystone Hospital in New Jersey, where he met the infirm Woody Guthrie, and to the East Orange home of Guthrie's friends Robert and Sidsel Gleason, where Guthrie was allowed to spend Sundays among the camaraderie of his folk-music friends. There Guthrie leaned against pillows while the others gathered around to talk and sing. Dylan shyly listened, occasionally approaching his idol to ask questions or sing songs. It was after his first trip out to the home in East Orange, around February 1961, that he wrote "Song to Woody," a rambling epic tribute to Guthrie's life and ideals.

Putting in long hours and exhaustive work, Dylan rose quickly within the New York music scene. Many people were drawn to the messages in his songs; some simply liked his unique, expressive singing style. Among the places he performed regularly were Gerde's Folk City and the Gaslight, both cafés that were especially popular with young people. It was at a performance at Gerde's Folk City in September 1961 that *New York Times* critic Robert Shelton, who was later to write a comprehensive biography of Dylan, first encountered him. It was Dylan's gravelly voice and self-confident demeanor that led Shelton to be the first critic to note an extraordinary talent. He gave the young singer a stellar review in the *New York Times,* stating that Dylan was "bursting at the seams with talent."

Woody Guthrie, a founding father of the American folk-music revival, is captured here in a 1943 photograph. Guthrie used his poignant voice to sing out in protest against injustice, especially when it was committed against the working class.

That review marked a turning point for Dylan. During the next month, while playing harmonica as accompaniment at a recording session for folksinger Carolyn Hester's album, he met John Hammond, an executive for Columbia Records, one of the major recording companies. Hammond was always on the lookout for new talent, and he responded to the young singer's conviction and musicality (and, possibly, to Shelton's *New York Times* review). By late October, Dylan had signed a recording contract with Columbia, and his debut album, called *Bob Dylan,* was released in March 1962.

The album was well received by listeners and critics alike, both in terms of Dylan's singing style and the songs he recorded. According to Michael Gray in *Song and Dance Man: The Art of Bob Dylan* (1981):

[The album] has such a young Dylan on it that he sounds about seventy-five. Only two of the songs are his own—one dedicated to his early idol Woody Guthrie (*Song to Woody*) and the other owing its whole format and spirit to Guthrie's own work (*Talkin' New York*).

The rest of the songs are mainly traditional and/or old blues songs by men like Jesse Fuller, Bukka White and Blind Lemon Jefferson. Dylan comes across as obsessed with the romance of dying, but the speed, energy and attack in his guitar, harmonica and voice show how fresh and excellently "unprofessional" he was.

Some of the songs were already known to those who listened to folk music. Songs such as "Pretty Peggy-O" or "House of the Rising Sun" had been performed for many years. But Dylan sang them in a way that caught a person's ear. His manner was not the clean, smooth crooning (such as that of pop artist Pat Boone) that dominated much of the popular music at the time. Dylan's voice was rough and uneven. He sometimes growled and other times almost talked. His guitar squawked and pounded, while his harmonica sighed and shrieked. Here was an artist who demanded attention.

"Talkin' New York" was loosely autobiographical, a talking blues narrative in the tradition of Guthrie in which Dylan talked/sang about city experiences, already showing the wry humor that was to become typical of him. In the song he blended current experiences in his life, making reference to the bitter cold of the winter of his arrival in New York City and adding a rhetorical twist by saying that once he heard it was the coldest winter in years, he did not feel quite so cold. The lyrics were a hint of the ironic wit to come.

Though people might have first noticed his rough-hewn singing style, it was the act of writing and performing his own songs that was to have a long-term effect on other musicians. In the early 1960s, most popular music was being written by professional songwriters, such as Jerry Leiber and Mike Stoller, or New York's Tin Pan Alley writers (to people like Dylan, Tin Pan Alley was a term used to refer to those composers and publishers who wrote shallow, slick music that was commercially popular), as well as Motown Record's Holland-Dozier-Holland team. Because songs were written by professional writers and then passed along, through a producer, to a singer who would record it, the acts of composing and performing were usually separated. Dylan, however, reintegrated the two phases. The first song of his own that he recorded for Columbia was "Song to Woody." By the time of his second album, *The Freewheelin' Bob Dylan,* released in 1963, Dylan was writing all of his own songs and performing them in his own idiosyncratic manner, beginning a tradition of the singer-songwriter that would inspire many subsequent musicians, including Carole King, Paul Simon, and Bruce Springsteen, and establish a new realm of possibility in popular music.

3 From Folk to Rock

GERDE'S FOLK CITY was a café, located at 11 West Fourth Street, in New York City's Greenwich Village. Gerde's had begun to sponsor concerts of folk music, called hootenannies, around 1960, and by the time Dylan began regularly appearing there, it had become a center for the folk-music revival and for liberal politics. During 1962 and 1963, Dylan played at Gerde's often, performing the songs he had written and rising to prominence in folk-music circles. It was at Gerde's, in April 1962, that he first performed a new song called "Blowin' in the Wind," which would soon reach a much wider audience than he had ever reached before. (It appeared on the front page of the underground newspaper *Broadside* in May, and then Peter, Paul and Mary made it a hit shortly before Dylan himself released the song on his second album in 1963.)

In *Bob Dylan: Behind the Shades* (1991), biographer Clinton Heylin wrote that Dylan prefaced the song by saying "This here ain't a protest song or anything like that, 'cause I don't write protest songs. . . . I'm just writing it as something to be said for somebody, by somebody." "Blowin' in the Wind"

In a Columbia Records studio, Dylan accompanies himself on the piano in June 1965. While living in New York in the early 1960s, Dylan said, "The words of the songs aren't written out just for the paper, they're written so you can read [them]. . . . It ain't the melodies that're important, man, it's the words."

had an anthemlike quality, with its simple four-line verses and use of symbolism. Like an anthem, it took poetic images, such as a man walking down a road or a dove flying, that, in their simplicity, were clearly about something other than themselves. Each line asked what was necessary to achieve understanding and resolution. The answer was close at hand, yet hard to define—it was "blowin' in the wind."

The song's wide popularity was symbolic of the prophetic figure that Dylan was becoming for more and more people. It was somehow appropriate, then, that in August 1962 Bob Zimmerman legally changed his name to Bob Dylan, making official the shift from Hibbing, Minnesota, to New York, New York, and from his middle-class midwestern roots to a unique voice that spoke outside of mainstream America. His artistic explorations and his focus on political and social issues brought Dylan into the public eye.

Dylan, who signed Albert Grossman up as his manager around this time, concentrated on writing his own songs, although he was deeply affected by the musical streams that swirled around him, and by factors in his personal life. His girlfriend, Suze Rotolo, whom he had met at a party after one of his gigs, was a powerful influence on him. Rotolo worked with the civil rights organization Congress of Racial Equality (CORE), and through her Dylan became even more aware of the struggle, particularly in the southern states, for equality and the desegregation of community facilities such as schools, restaurants, and public transportation. Rotolo's older sister, Carla, was an ardent fan

A view inside the Gaslight Café, a popular hangout for New York City's Beatniks, shows a young woman reciting poetry in 1959. When Dylan arrived in Greenwich Village in 1961, he often performed with other folksingers at the Gaslight.

of Dylan's and worked for Alan Lomax, one of the most celebrated authorities of American folk music. Dylan had access to Carla's record collection and to the Rotolos' and other friends' libraries, which included the works of German playwright Bertolt Brecht, the French poet Arthur Rimbaud, and the British poet T. S. Eliot. Deeply attached to Suze, Dylan asked her to move into his West Fourth Street apartment in December 1961. Eve MacKenzie, who had befriended Dylan when he first arrived in the Village, told Heylin that "Suze . . . wanted [Dylan] to go Pete Seeger's way. She wanted Bobby to be involved in civil rights and all the radical causes Seeger was involved in. Suze was very much with the cause. . . . She influenced Bobby considerably that way." Suze also brought stability to Dylan, but in June 1962 she left for Italy to study painting. Dylan, lonely and anxious in New York, immersed himself in writing love songs.

In May 1963, the results of his lovelorn explorations appeared on his second album, *The Freewheelin' Bob Dylan*. From the noble "Blowin' in the Wind" to the evocative ballad "Girl from the North Country," Dylan's songs were truly his own on this record. The musical style and the lyrics were reflective of the personality that was emerging from the amalgam of musical styles he heard around him. In 1963, Dylan said of *Freewheelin'*: "There's too many old-fashioned songs in there, stuff I tried to write like Woody. I'm goin' through changes. Need some more finger-pointin' songs in it, 'cause that's where my head's at right now." If, on his first album, he had been sampling the different personas of folk music and the blues, with the second he had become himself.

Dylan tackled current political issues on the album, but in a way that explored the deep personal convictions that are carried with them. "Blowin' in the Wind" set these beliefs into a universal hymn, becoming an icon for an entire generation that searched for something better

Suze Rotolo watches Dylan rehearse for his first Columbia recording session in 1961. Rotolo, a political activist, was Dylan's girlfriend from 1961 to 1964, and she inspired some of Dylan's most touching love songs.

in life. In the song "Masters of War," Dylan deals with the topic of war once again but in a much more outspoken way, and he bitterly criticizes the insulation of arms manufacturers and politicians from the effect of the weapons they produce and deploy. Dubbing these militarists "masters of war," he refers to their guns and bombs and to their taking refuge behind walls and desks, and says that, though they might believe they are safely behind the scenes, their guilt is nonetheless obvious. In the last verse of the song, Dylan mercilessly wishes for their destruction, swearing that he will stand over their graves until he is certain they are dead.

This final verse is not a description of war but an acidic judgment of those behind it, and it moved far beyond the usual boundaries of socially oriented folk music. Traditional folk songs usually tell a story or speak about a universal human experience, such as love, marriage, or death. But Dylan examined the *personal* experience and conviction behind social and political events. He not only remarked on a particular topic, such as war in "Masters of War" or racially motivated murder in "The Death of Emmett Till," but he offered a heavy-handed judgment of the perpetrators of these "crimes" as well. This sense of moral imperative, though presented on the album as social concern, was typical of Dylan and would later take shape in other forms, such as Christian discipleship in the 1970s. Such moral commentary, which Dylan expressed poignantly, passionately, and concisely, spoke to an entire generation and pushed *Freewheelin'* into the realm of popular music. The album transcended the smaller New York folk-music circles with which Dylan had been identified, touching people who were less interested in the folk-music movement and who simply responded to Dylan's image, his unusual sound, and his fresh convictions.

In the tradition of Woody Guthrie and others, such as Pete Seeger, who had combined music and social action and resisted what they felt to be unjust governmental policy, Dylan became more and more politically active in a public way. On May 12, 1963, he was scheduled to appear on the widely popular television show, "The Ed Sullivan Show." The song he had rehearsed to perform that night was his "Talkin' John Birch Paranoid Blues," a biting satire about conservative politics. But just before Dylan was to go onstage, he was told that, because of the controversial nature of the song, he would have to choose another one to sing. Rather than change his plans at the last minute, he simply walked out of the studio. In May, Dylan also appeared with folksinger Joan Baez at the Monterey Folk Festival in California, and in July, he performed at the Newport Folk Festival with Baez and the folk group Peter, Paul and Mary, just when the latter's version of "Blowin' in the Wind" moved to the top of the popular music charts. His appearance there cemented his image as the darling of the folk-music movement, with help from Baez, who was considered to be the queen of folk and who had recently become romantically involved with Dylan. Joan Baez told Heylin years later, "I was getting audiences of up to ten thousand at that point, and dragging my little vagabond out onto the stage was a grand experiment. . . . The people who had not heard of Bob were often infuriated and sometimes even booed him." In the summer of 1963, he sang at a civil rights rally in Greenwood, Mississippi, and on August 28, in the massive civil rights demonstration in Washington, D.C., where Martin Luther King, Jr., gave his powerful "I Have a Dream" speech.

In January 1964, Dylan released his third album, *The Times They Are A-Changin'*, the songs of which explored social inequality on several different levels. Whereas "Blowin' in the Wind" had been an anthem, the title song of the new album became a rallying cry. It left behind simpler poetic couplets and classic symbols for more irregular verses and disturbing images about such notions as the rising tidewaters that can overtake and drown those who cannot swim, and about those who cannot leave behind outmoded social codes for newer, more inclusive ones. The youth of America also considered the song to be about the generation gap, but Dylan later squashed this view when he said, "It happened that maybe those were the only words I could find to separate aliveness from deadness. It had nothing to do with age." "The Lonesome Death of Hattie Carroll" and "The Ballad of Hollis Brown" sketched out specific examples of social injustice but were more than just storytelling: for example, Hattie Carroll, an African-American maid, is senselessly murdered by a rich white man who beat her with his cane because she was slow in bringing him a drink. Dylan went beyond the issues of Hattie's servitude and murder and suggested that the truest sin lay in the negligible sentence given to her affluent killer. Dylan's "With God on Our Side" was an ironic portrait of the simplistic way in which people are taught to accept and believe in war. He reproves those who use religion to justify the use of violence. Some songs on the album merely captured personal moments. For instance, "One Too Many Mornings" describes an impasse between two lovers and preludes Dylan's deeper personal focus on albums to come. Yet Dylan's third record demonstrated that popular music, although a social force in the 1950s, had now become a form of social action.

For many people, however, that call for action was becoming synonymous with Dylan himself, a role he had never sought for himself. It seemed as though Dylan, who had only been a participant in a movement, now found himself its head. In light of the slickly produced, purposefully innocuous pop stars of the day, such as Lesley Gore, Bobby Vinton, Andy Williams, and—at least in the early 1960s—the Beatles, it was not only unusual but powerful to hear such a gifted musician speak harshly yet poetically about contemporary social issues, and fans looked to Dylan for inspiration. But the cloak of "hero" began to weigh heavily on him. Dylan became more cutting and curt than a public hero should be, and he baffled many fans. In March 1964, his relationship with Suze Rotolo ended. Years later, Rotolo told Heylin,

> We were young and vulnerable. A lot of crazy things happened . . . because of his growing fame. . . . He began snubbing his old friends. But it was all so understandable in an odd way. He could see these things happening to him and he wanted to make sure they would happen, so at the same time he didn't have time to just hang out anymore. He was working on his image and his career. . . . I don't think he wanted me to do anything separate from him. He wanted me to be completely one hundred percent a part of what he was. He was tied up with his own development, and it was just his world that became concentrated in just music.

Uncomfortable with being in the spotlight and with all of the expectations that fame had heaped upon him, he gradually began to move toward the edge.

Striking evidence of Dylan's resistance to assuming others' expectations came in the form of his next record, *Another Side of Bob Dylan,* which was released in August 1964. Both in musical style and in lyrics, he took new directions, unquestionably asserting his need to pursue his own ideas. He still wove political consciousness into the themes of his songs. But more than the specific topical references of his previous lyrics and the sense of indictment that often accompanied them, Dylan began to go beyond even his own boundaries, expressing deep irony and pathos within scenarios that were not clear-cut but rather metaphorical. For example, the second verse of "My Back Pages" alluded to discrimination, but in a way that was not so much accusational as simply agonized. Prejudice and hate are wrong, but the complexities that give rise to them become too difficult to fathom and judge. The images Dylan used were increasingly surreal, unrelated to any coherent real-life situation, and led the way to the abstract lyrics of his mid-1960s albums.

Nat Hentoff of the *New Yorker* magazine interviewed Dylan on June 9, 1964, the same day Dylan recorded his fourth album, and Dylan talked about the constraints the songs imposed on him:

> It's hard being free in a song—getting it all in. Songs are so confining. . . . A song has to have some kind of form to fit into the music. You can bend the words and the meter, but it still has to fit somehow. I've been getting freer in the songs I write, but I still feel confined. That's why I write a lot of poetry, if that's the word. Poetry can make its own form.

Dylan went on to explain, "There aren't any finger-pointing songs in here. . . . Those records I've made, I'll stand behind them, but some of that was jumping into the scene to be heard and a lot of it was because I didn't see anybody else doing that kind of thing. . . . You know—pointing to all the things that are wrong. Me, I don't want to write *for* people anymore. You know—be a spokesman. From now on, I want to write from inside me, and to do that I'm going to have to get back to writing like I used to when I was ten—having everything come out naturally. The way I like to write is for it to come out the way I walk or talk."

The musical style on *Another Side* eclipsed a simpler folk-music orientation and suggested the fuller texture—more musical lines being played at once—and volume that were more akin to rock music. Indeed, the final song, "It Ain't Me, Babe," was seen by many to be an explicit refutation of the folk-music role that had been handed to him. The lyrics seemingly referred to the singer's rejection of a lover whose expectations were too confining and idealized, expectations that could just as aptly apply to the folk-movement audience he had already left behind. For Dylan, the protest movement was dead. He told songwriter Phil Ochs, "The stuff you're writing is bullshit, because politics is bullshit. It's all unreal. The only thing that's real is inside you. Your feelings. Just look at the world you're writing about and you'll see you're wasting your time. The world is, well . . . it's just absurd."

Press conferences, important to a musician's career since the beginning of rock, reflected Dylan's evasiveness, too. His interviews were becoming increasingly unpredictable and, occasionally, abrasive, as his own honesty and comfort during them failed to keep up with the demands of a music-business image. Interviews with the press were not the perfunctory, harmless public appearances of some celebrities, but rather situations in which Dylan used wit and will to maintain control over the journalists. In a press conference on December 3, 1965, for WQED-TV in San Francisco, Dylan continually and somewhat sarcastically thwarted the probing questions he was asked:

Dylan and Joan Baez, the queen of folk music during the 1960s, are photographed in London, England, in April 1965, prior to the breakup of their affair. With Baez's backing at the 1963 Newport Folk Festival, Dylan became a star.

Press: Do you think of yourself primarily as a singer or a poet?

Dylan: Oh, I think of myself more as a song-and-dance man.

Press: [music journalist] Josh Dunson . . . implies that you have sold out to commercial interests . . .

Dylan: . . . I sincerely don't feel guilty.

Press: If you were going to sell out to a commercial interest, which one would you choose?

Dylan: Ladies garments. . . .

Press: What are your own personal hopes for the future and what do you hope to change in the world?

Dylan: I don't have any hopes for the future and I just hope to have enough boots to be able to change them.

Press: Why do you think you're so popular?

Dylan: I don't know. I'm not a reporter. I'm not a newsman . . . I'm not even a philosopher, so I have no idea.

Of course, Dylan actually *was* a philosopher, singer, and poet. But his sparring with the media was evasive and self-protective. Dylan had risen from being a popular musician to being a pop idol.

The album that he released in March 1965—many of the songs of which he had written while staying at the Grossmans' house in Woodstock, New York—helped to cement the transition. With *Bringin' It All Back Home,* Dylan fully developed the style of a rock music that was based on the blues, a particularly radical step for someone who had been seen as the earnest spokesman of a folk movement. In particular, he had begun to experiment with the use of electric instruments, such as the electric guitar and organ. In an almost aggressive statement of the vision that he was pursuing, half the songs on the album used electric instruments, with an emphasis on the style and sound of rhythm-and-blues music. The other side of the album was all acoustic. His lyrics made fewer overt references to politics and dealt instead with poetic impressions of the life (including politics) around him. The first track, "Subterranean Homesick Blues," used a blues band, with electric bass and guitar, drums and vocals, and the form of the song—rapid and somewhat nonsensical rhyming couplets—had often been used by rhythm-and-blues performers. In this forceful song, Dylan warns youth not to trust established authorities. The 15 verses and 5 refrains of "It's Alright, Ma (I'm Only Bleeding)," make clear that Dylan was still concerned about social issues, and that he had to experience them not in terms of a public movement, but in a confused and uncontrollable search for integrity. Many critics believe the song is the masterpiece of the album; in it, Dylan confronts the generation conflict once again. Wayne Hampton, in his 1986 book *Guerrilla Minstrels,* describes the theme of the song.

> "Ma," of course, symbolizes the older generation, the establishment, tradition, and authority. To Ma, Dylan (representing youth) tries to explain himself and the dehumanizing and alienating conditions that have forced him and his peers to reject everything. . . . Face it, says Dylan, your world has gone crazy, the system is disintegrating. . . . There is no point trying to make sense of anything. . . . Only the inner experience of feeling and euphoria can lead one out of alienation and pain; rationalism and commitment of traditional ideologies are the paths of the dead.

The final songs on the album are folklike in their form and use of acoustic instruments, but their imagery is mystical and evocative. Though it contains no clear-cut references to specific drugs, many people thought at the time that the ethereal "Mr. Tambourine Man" was based on the use of hallucinogens, such as LSD.

Bringin' It All Back Home enchanted some fans and disturbed others, and people began to pay closer attention to Dylan's every move. Other musicians clearly felt his influence. Some were beginning to "cover" his songs,

Dylan plays a Fender bass guitar for an advertisement for Fender instruments, circa 1965. Dylan had experimented with electric instruments before he recorded *Bringin' It All Back Home* in January 1965; it was also around this time that he decided to use a backup band.

performing in their own style the pieces that he had already recorded. In 1964, the rock group the Animals had recorded "House of the Rising Sun," a traditional song that Dylan had made popular on his first album, and in the summer of 1965, the Byrds would hit the pop charts with "Mr. Tambourine Man" (which Dylan had written in May 1964). In August 1964, in New York City, Dylan first met the other rising giants in pop music, the Beatles. Though this was their first formal introduction, George Harrison later remembered that Dylan had been an influence on them long before they actually met: "The day Bob Dylan really turned us on was the day we heard his album, *The Freewheelin' Bob Dylan.* Right from

46

that moment we recognized some vital energy, a voice crying out somewhere, toiling in the darkness. When we actually met him in '64 it had a certain effect on us, but I think the seed was already sown by the album."

Clearly, Dylan's influence and popularity had spread well beyond U.S. borders to Great Britain. In April and May 1965, he toured there, just predating the "British invasion," when English rock groups flooded the American pop music charts. Documentary filmmaker D. A. Pennebaker went along with Dylan on his short trip through England (this was his third trip; Dylan had visited England briefly in mid-December 1962 and again in May 1964), recorded it, and released it as the 90-minute movie *Don't Look Back,* filmed in black and white. The opening of the movie is a sequence showing Dylan standing in a London alley, with two men in the background (one of them is Beat poet-philosopher Allen Ginsberg). "Subterranean Homesick Blues," from *Bringin' It All Back Home,* plays while Dylan holds a series of large white cards that have the last word of each line of the song written on them. As each line goes by, he pulls off that card, revealing the one beneath. This scenario quickly became well known and was an early example of combining a rock song with drama on film—preceding the 1980s music videos of MTV.

The rest of the movie takes a straightforward look at the kinds of situations that came up during the tour. Pennebaker filmed contractual negotiations, press interviews, concert footage, and casual backstage interactions, including those with folksinger Joan Baez, with whom Dylan was just ending an affair. Much of the music that Dylan performs, such as "The Lonesome Death of Hattie Carroll" and "The Times They Are A-Changin'," was still folk oriented, but his command of huge audiences and his own self-description in which he denied he was a folk artist pointed toward Dylan's arrival at a new plateau of

47

stardom. All of the situations are colored by Dylan's characteristic ambiguity and irony, particularly in scenes where he duals mercilessly with journalists. What emerges in the film is the life of Dylan as the star he had become, a tribute both to the difficulty of his life and the self-consciousness that such high visibility engendered.

D. A. Pennebaker later explained to Clinton Heylin that he realized there was a transformation of Dylan taking place:

> There was the problem of sticking with Dylan, who was under a number of pressures, including those from Joan Baez (personal) and the concerts (public). I had to take it on faith the film would not be a series of press conferences and getting in and out of concert halls. . . . It became clear that Dylan was going through some kind of change, and I knew that if I could stick with him I'd see something of it.

The tension between Dylan's huge popularity, his need for privacy, and the new directions suggested in his recent songs set the stage for the explosive two years that were to follow and that were ignited by one key event during the summer of 1965. On July 24–25, Dylan returned to the Newport Folk Festival, where, for the preceding two years, he had been so enthusiastically received in the company of Pete Seeger, Peter, Paul and Mary, and Joan Baez. But Dylan knew that time had passed; he had changed, and he was going to give the audience a taste of that metamorphosis. The music of *Bringin' It All Back Home* had begun to sound more like rock and roll, and Dylan decided to reveal his new direction by asking the Paul Butterfield Blues Band to serve as his backup players—a band that played *electric* guitar and bass, instead of the quieter and more traditional acoustic instruments. The distinction was a very important one to many folk-music fans, who preferred the acoustic guitar and believed that anyone who used electric instruments would be committing the ultimate sacrilege toward folk music.

Dylan and his new band had stayed up all night before their performance rehearsing their act, and they told no one about their plan. The audience waited with happy anticipation for Dylan to appear, and fans greeted him warmly, expecting to hear the latest visionary folk songs, or their favorite old ones, by the musical prophet from whom they had come to expect so much. But instead of singing "Blowin' in the Wind" with his acoustic guitar and harmonica, Dylan and the band lit into a fully electric version of "Maggie's Farm," in a style that was not folk at all, but rock. The audience resisted immediately, heckling and booing during the performance. The band went on to play "Like a Rolling Stone," but the audience had become so hostile, and the boos so loud, that they finally left the stage. Dylan appeared once more and calmed the audience by playing "It's All Over Now, Baby Blue" and "Mr. Tambourine Man" with simple guitar and harmonica. The latter song was a popular favorite, but the former, purposeful and explicit: Dylan as icon of the folk-music movement no longer existed. He was clearly going his own way, and the folk audience, as well as the broader popular one, could only guess at what was to come.

Filmmaker D. A. Pennebaker records a pensive Dylan aboard a train in England during Dylan's 1965 tour. Pennebaker's documentary, entitled *Don't Look Back,* includes Dylan performing live onstage, singing in hotel rooms with Joan Baez and Donovan, being interviewed by the press, and arguing with his entourage.

4 A Star

I N 1965 AND 1966, Dylan released three of the most notable albums of his career. *Bringin' It All Back Home* had come out in March 1965, *Highway 61 Revisited* appeared in August, and *Blonde on Blonde* was released in May 1966. But two significant personal events also occurred during this time: he first encountered and began to work with the rock group called the Hawks (later renamed the Band), and on November 22, 1965 he married Sara Lowndes.

If *Bringin' It All Back Home* had been a transition to a blues-based rock, then *Highway 61 Revisited,* which came out just after the Newport Folk Festival, was rock music. The ensemble sounded less like a blues group and more like a modern rock band, with clearer definition of the individual lines of the different instruments. The album, which took its name from the highway that runs through Duluth and Minneapolis, Minnesota, was headed up by the song "Like a Rolling Stone," which, with its ebullient indignation and solid backbeat, has become the quintessential rock song. Its wailing electric organ was played by Al Kooper, a talented young performer who

Dylan goofs off at the Hôtel Georges V in Paris, France, in May 1966. The publicity around his sold-out Paris concert was intense; the French newspaper *France-Soir* sarcastically called Dylan "Champion of the Singing Beatniks."

continued to play with Dylan for several years and helped him produce some of his later records. "Tombstone Blues" and "From a Buick 6" used a rhythm-and-blues-based style, much like that of Chuck Berry, or the early Rolling Stones, who had recorded their own versions of American blues songs from the 1950s. In "Desolation Row," which concludes the album, the use of unamplified guitar was a nod to Dylan's acoustical past, but in form and content it was what some critics called a "poem-song." In a rambling series of rich but fragmented images, Dylan seems to wander along the edges of society, no longer suggesting moral guidelines but merely observing the struggle. Of the song, biographer Anthony Scaduto states,

> It is a descent into a modern Inferno, an eleven-minute freak show that portrays a world of alienation ruled by madmen, a world in which humanity has been estranged from its own possibilities, a world in which man's once free mind has been so totally suffocated by the one dimensional society that it accepts lies as truth and beauty, permits creativity and naturalness and Eros to be perverted by the social "reality." Not since Rimbaud has a poet used the language of the streets to expose all the horrors of the streets, to describe a state of the union that is ugly and absurd.

Highway 61 Revisited was considered to be at that time one of the most important and brilliant popular music albums ever made. Dylan was pleased with the record, his first all-rock album, and in 1966 said, "I'm not gonna be able to make a record better than that one. 'Highway 61' is just too good. There's a lot of stuff on there that I would listen to."

In August 1965, Dylan met up with a young Canadian-based band called the Hawks, whose members included guitarist Robbie Robertson, drummer Levon Helm, bassist Rick Danko, pianist Richard Manuel, and organist Garth Hudson. The Hawks had been working as a backup band in Toronto for a singer named Ronnie Hawkins, and Dylan first heard them in a bar in New Jersey while he was looking around for musicians to help him play his new electric brand of rock. He immediately knew that this was the group with which he wanted to work. Their rhythm-and-blues based, country-influenced electric rock offered what Dylan felt he was ready for, and his folk background and unique musical inspiration gave the Hawks an opportunity to enhance their own distinctive style. They began working together immediately.

Robbie Robertson, on electric lead guitar, and Levon Helm, on drums, played with Dylan in his first perform-ance with his own rock band on August 28, 1965. The concert was held at the Forest Hills Tennis Stadium in Queens, New York. The event got off to a rocky start when Dylan was introduced, not by a regular announcer, but by Murray the K (Kaufman), a pop music disc jockey, who, to the stadium audience, declared, "It's not rock, it's not folk, it's a new thing called Dylan!" Dylan's first set of songs was acoustic—for 45 minutes he appeared onstage alone, with just his guitar and harmonica. He sang "She Belongs to Me," "Ramona," "Gates of Eden," "Love Minus Zero," "Desolation Row," "Baby Blue," and "Mr. Tambourine Man." But Dylan's second set was electric, and he and the band played "Maggie's Farm," "Ballad of a Thin Man," "It Ain't Me, Babe," and "Like a Rolling Stone," among other songs. The audience reacted angrily, booing the performers; a few even threw fruit. Years later, Al Kooper talked to Heylin about that Forest Hills performance: "[Dylan] knew something was gonna happen because he gave us like a pep talk before the show. He said, 'Now, there's gonna be some kinda circus out there. Just ignore whatever happens and play the show.' He knew something was gonna happen."

Sara Lowndes married Bob Dylan on November 22, 1965. She is seen here in 1969 with her husband at Heathrow Airport in London, England. Many of Dylan's friends were surprised by his secret marriage to Lowndes.

Dylan adamantly threw himself into the electric music at the Forest Hills concert and many more. The rest of the Hawks' members joined Dylan for his 1965–66 world tour, which included such cities as Los Angeles, California, in September, New York City in October, Toronto, Canada, in November, and San Francisco in December.

Throughout this time, Dylan's personal life, though often hinted at in some of his songs, had never been fully disclosed. Some rock stars made a public statement about their wedding ceremonies or intimate affairs, but Dylan, whose philanderings were generally known only by his closest friends, did not. Few people knew that he had met a young woman named Sara Shirley Lowndes, who had once been a *Playboy* bunny and had been previously married and had a daughter, Maria. According to biographer Robert Shelton, "[Dylan] admired her inner resources, her quietude, and philosophic calm, her ability to be herself, with or without him." Sara had been introduced to Dylan by Sally Grossman, the wife of his manager. Sara had visited Dylan frequently at Woodstock, had joined him at the end of his tour in England in April 1965, and had gone on a brief vacation with him in Portugal. In November, in an unannounced ceremony in New York State, Dylan married Sara, the quiet, striking young woman with whom he had so quickly fallen in love. Few knew about the wedding. The press only found out about the marriage in the days following, and throughout their marriage, Sara remained private and somewhat detached from her husband's public life.

That winter, Dylan continued his world tour with the Hawks, and in April 1966 they went to Australia. Dylan and his new band liked playing together and were developing a good rapport. Yet the tour was wearying for the group; not only was travel tiring, but audiences were still strained and hostile. Between concerts, Dylan found time to stop in Nashville, Tennessee, the center of the country music scene. In a Nashville studio, he recorded the songs for his next album, *Blonde on Blonde,* which he had been working on for several months. Once in the recording studio, Dylan traditionally worked fairly quickly, often recording several songs in one evening. Many rock groups, such as the Beatles, spent months editing and producing their songs in a recording studio. Dylan, however, loved improvisation and spontaneity during his sessions, and his method of working epitomized his insistence on doing the recordings in a manner that *he* felt comfortable with. Allen Ginsberg later explained Dylan's work habits to Heylin:

On May 1, 1966, Dylan visited Kronborg Castle in Helsingør, "City of Hamlet," Denmark. That same year, Dylan took a break from his world tour with the Hawks and recorded *Blonde on Blonde* in a Nashville, Tennessee, studio.

Dylan always did improvise quite a bit. . . . 'Round '65 he told me that . . . he used to go into a studio and chat up the musicians and babble into the microphone, then rush into the control room and listen to what he said, and write it down, and then maybe arrange it a little bit, and then maybe rush back out in front and sing it!

The album *Blonde on Blonde* was released to the public in May 1966, and it took the rich rhythm-and-blues-based music and the poetic world of the earlier two albums one step further. Twelve years after the album's release, Dylan said,

Poet Allen Ginsberg of the Beat Generation reads a poem to a crowd in New York's Washington Square Park in August 1966. Ginsberg first met Dylan in 1963, and they have remained friends ever since. Ginsberg appeared in the opening sequence of Pennebaker's *Don't Look Back*.

The closest I ever got to the sound I hear in my mind was on individual bands in the "Blonde on Blonde" album. It's that thin, that wild mercury sound. It's metallic and bright gold, with whatever that conjures up. That's my particular sound. I haven't been able to succeed in getting it all the time. Mostly I've been driving at a combination of guitar, harmonica and organ.

The opening song, "Rainy Day Women #12 & 35," is one of Dylan's most well known and became a symbol of mid-1960s youth. Over a rollicking and loose instrumental ensemble, Dylan jokingly characterized the drug

culture, with a seemingly endless play on the idea of being "stoned" on drugs. The final line of each verse reiterated that "Everybody must get stoned." Given the climate of a youth counterculture that was, in part, defined by its interest in experimentation with various types of drugs, Dylan's song became controversial, and some radio stations went so far as to ban it.

The rest of the album delved more deeply into songs about impressionistic personal experiences and intimate relationships. "Visions of Johanna," a seven-and-a-half-minute song, wandered through fragmented images of time and place that were tied together with mysterious evocations of a woman named "Johanna." (Many people believe the song's Johanna represented Joan Baez, with whom Dylan had ended an affair.) Like the French symbolist poetry of Arthur Rimbaud that Dylan had earlier been fascinated by, the lyrics merged the different senses, such as smell, touch, and sound, into one experience, as when heat, country music, flickering lights, and "lovers entwined" merge into one blurred scene. But rather than simply painting a sweet, sensual picture, the lyrics are skewed with denial, defiance, and uncertainty. The result is one of the most notable of Dylan's songs, a pastiche of open-ended impressions framed by the consistent return of Johanna. Critics have singled out this love song as one of Dylan's masterpieces, calling it "haunting" and perhaps his "most perfect song."

Other songs on *Blonde on Blonde* seem to have been more clearly inspired by Sara, such as "Sad-Eyed Lady of the Lowlands," regarded by many as one of Dylan's most beautiful love songs. According to Robert Shelton, Dylan considered this song, which ends the album, to be "the best song I ever wrote." The folklike ballad uses the symbolic imagery that has become typical of Dylan, where things and ideas that seem incoherent and nonsensical, but arouse an air of mystery, warmth, and sadness, surround an unnamed woman to whom the singer addresses his questions. *Sing-Out!* editor Paul Nelson referred to Dylan's song as a "celebration of woman as work of art, religious figure, and object of eternal majesty and wonder."

The lyrics of *Blonde on Blonde,* together with *Bringin' It All Back Home* and *Highway 61 Revisited,* struck a powerful balance between, on the one hand, being very individual and subjective and, on the other, being relevant to a wide variety of people. Dylan's use of metaphor was sophisticated and often obscure, as in the cycle of ideas in "Visions of Johanna," and his vocabulary combined poetic images with everyday language and blunt, unpoetical emotions. He both conceived of and delivered humor as effectively as tragedy, frequently intertwining the two. Dylan's unique use of narrative—telling a story over the course of a song—had, by now, definitively changed the more objective style that was typical of folk music into a more personal, impressionistic one, colored by all the richness that he felt in the world around him. Dylan proved that rock music could be serious music, intellectual and poetic, and at the same time meaningful to many people. He broke ground that no one else had even envisioned until then, laying to rest any contention folk-music purists could have had that rock was somehow less serious or less socially important than folk music.

Rock lyrics, originally artful "fun" in the rock and roll of the 1950s, had become a social message in the early 1960s, in great part as a result of Dylan's efforts. But now Dylan himself had expanded that idea of lyrics even further, to rich, rambling poetic explorations that did not fit into the typical outlines of a three-minute pop song. Dylan, along with groups like the Beatles and the Beach Boys, took rock to a new level. Songs could be short or long; they could include wry irony, sarcasm, desolation, or joy, and the topic of love was no longer confined to

teenage infatuation but was treated from all the angles of mature experience. The rock album became an artistic commodity that fell into the hands of anxiously awaiting youth, who perceived it not only as entertainment but as guidance as well.

The musical style of *Blonde on Blonde, Bringin' It All Back Home,* and *Highway 61 Revisited* reached a high point of melodic expression, fusing together elements of rock, folk, and blues into a unique language that Dylan would draw on for all his later albums. This merging of various musical styles has since come to be known as "folk rock" and has been associated with performers such as the Byrds. However, in these albums Dylan did not really

In Paris, France, in May 1966, Dylan, with his puppet Finian (far right) seated beside him, shows his intolerance of the press, whom he believed always asked the wrong questions. He told the French reporters, "I don't belong to any movement. I've only got some ideas in my head and I tell them. I don't support anybody's cause. No revolution ever came about because of songs."

59

create a subcategory of rock. Instead, he brought new musical elements into mainstream rock and changed the direction of popular music in general. Dylan's music on these three albums elicited a wide range of responses from fans. Some, who still identified with Dylan's early folk-music days, felt that he had sold out to commercial interests, betraying his personal ideals for the sake of a popular audience. Others saw the three albums as a brilliant consummation of folk, rock, poetry, and blues, a culmination that was pure Dylan.

By the summer of 1966, Dylan's career had come to a fervent climax, eclipsing his folk-movement beginnings and producing a rich and unusual trio of albums. He and the Hawks had returned from their world tour in May. They were exhausted and discouraged; audiences still had very mixed reactions to the new folk rock, sometimes cheering but often booing, and Dylan and his band frequently had trouble properly adjusting the amplification produced by the electric sound system onstage. They had given many concerts, their schedule made even more taxing by their heavy use of alcohol and drugs. But despite their fatigue, manager Albert Grossman had already lined up for the musicians a series of equally tiring concerts in the United States. In June, in an effort to briefly escape the unforgiving pressure of Dylan's career, Dylan and Sara quietly slipped away to the one place where he had consistently found rejuvenation: Woodstock.

Since 1963, Dylan had come to spend more and more time in this small village nestled in the Catskill Mountains in upstate New York. First introduced to it by Peter Yarrow of Peter, Paul and Mary, he was immediately attracted to the quiet starry nights, the lush, damp vegetation, and the crystal air. In 1969, Woodstock would become known as the site of an immense three-day rock festival (the 1969 music and art fair was actually held on a farm in nearby Bethel), but its cultural roots went far deeper than that. Beginning in the early 20th century, it had been a retreat for artists, writers, and musicians, as well as for a few wealthy New Yorkers who would escape to its woods during the summer. When Dylan first came to know it, it was not yet in the public consciousness.

However, this trip to Woodstock proved to take Dylan farther than he had anticipated. On July 29, 1966, while skimming along damp roads on his Triumph motorcycle, the rear wheels locked and Dylan went flying over the handlebars. He was rushed to the hospital, and though news of his accident quickly spread, no one knew, or has ever known, exactly how severely he was hurt. There were reports of broken vertebrae and of a concussion, and for months Dylan slowly recovered at his Woodstock home, inaccessible to the public, with Sara and their son, Jesse, who had been born the previous month. His intense career came spiraling to a halt as concerts were immediately canceled. Whatever the specific nature of his injuries, Dylan's accident gave him the opportunity—the seclusion and the breathing space—to step back from the expectations that were put upon him, to spend time with his family, and to reevaluate his life and his music.

5 Beyond Rock

OR THE NEXT TWO YEARS, while the popular music world spiraled upward around him, Dylan remained isolated in Woodstock. It was a chance for him to take charge once again of his own musical explorations, and the members of the Hawks, who had changed their name to the Band in the spring of 1968, came up to join him. They rented a small pink house in West Saugerties, New York, a few minutes away from Woodstock, and in the basement, Dylan and the Band made new music, an event that has become one of the most celebrated in rock history. From June to October 1967, they experimented, improvised—played spontaneously, without using music that was written down—wrote new songs and played traditional ones. Dylan would often work late into the night, coming up with a new piece and calling the band members in to try it out. The hippie movement, psychedelia, and the San Francisco sound of the 1968 "Summer of Love" went on around them, with rock bands such as the Grateful Dead and Jefferson Airplane

Elliot Landy's photograph captured a happy Bob Dylan at Dylan's home in Woodstock, New York. This image was used for the cover of Dylan's album *Nashville Skyline,* which was released in April 1969.

improvising very long and highly amplified songs while both audience and performers were under the influence of the drug LSD. But Dylan and his fellow musicians were lost in a quieter music of their own.

The music they recorded at Big Pink (the name they gave the pink house in West Saugerties) was originally meant to be for a demo, a recording that is produced quickly and only to serve as a demonstration of what a polished performance in a real recording studio might sound like. But Dylan decided not to have the material officially released, and for years bootleg tapes—tapes illegally made without Dylan's approval and outside of the usual music-business channels—circulated among Dylan's fans. Other rock musicians, such as singer-guitarist Eric Clapton, who were lucky enough to come across such tapes were profoundly affected by the new music. Some bands even covered songs from the tapes, such as Peter, Paul and Mary's rendition of "Too Much of Nothing" and Manfred Mann's version of "The Mighty Quinn (Quinn the Eskimo)." But the general public had its first chance to hear the music only in July 1975, when 24 of the Big Pink songs were released as an album entitled *The Basement Tapes.* The album features some of Dylan's best-known songs, including "I Shall Be Released," "This Wheel's on Fire," "Tears of Rage," and "Sign of the Cross."

In hindsight, the album's release revealed that, at the height of the 1960s cultural bang and, in particular, just when the hugely influential *Sgt. Pepper's Lonely Hearts Club Band* had been released by the Beatles, Dylan completely dodged the tenor of the times and ducked into a world of his own. Tucked away with his fellow musicians in a little-known area in upstate New York, he once again followed his own musical intuition, even though it ran counter to what fans and the music business would have either liked or anticipated from him. Dylan had moved away from the longer poem-songs of his albums from the mid-1960s and returned to more traditional forms, not only folk music but country, early rock and roll, gospel, and ballads. The songs were heartfelt, intense, often calm, and unrelated to so much of what was going on around him.

In the use of these unadorned musical styles, *The Basement Tapes* also provided evidence of a crucial link in Dylan's development. Prior to his motorcycle accident, the trilogy of *Bringin' It All Back Home, Highway 61 Revisited,* and *Blonde on Blonde* had reached an apex of complexity in the style and length of the music and in the poetic messages of the lyrics. Politics had become only fleeting allusion in the strange pictures the songs painted, and many of the images, in their surreal quality and odd juxtapositions with each other, had suggested psychedelia, or drug-related distortions of reality. But suddenly, in January 1968, fans who had anxiously awaited a follow-up to *Blonde on Blonde* got *John Wesley Harding* instead.

On the quiet album *John Wesley Harding,* the songs are simple, relatively short, and inspired most clearly by the style of country music. Beside the complexity of Dylan's 1966 albums, *John Wesley Harding* seemed sparse. The album's title, also the name of the first song, referred to the 19th-century outlaw of the American West, John Wesley Hardin (Dylan added the *g*). Dylan told Hardin's story in the form of a brief parable, painting Hardin as a Robin Hood–like figure who was just and moral, but who was also an outsider. Dylan's gun-toting Harding befriended the poor, recognizing and protecting those who were inherently honest. Yet the short, plain song did not paint a full picture of a misunderstood outlaw but rather left him undefined and mysterious, a savvy and elusive character who could well have been an analogy for Dylan himself at that point.

"All Along the Watchtower" also spoke of societal boundaries but without as clear a sense of right and wrong as "John Wesley Harding" suggested. After a powerful opening by the guitar and harmonica, a joker and a thief converse briefly. They imply, though never clarify, the confinement and confusion they feel within some sort of fortress, or society, that is set apart by the watchtower from whatever lies beyond it. Both the joker and the thief describe things that make some sense on a literal level but are obviously symbolic of something else. The joker, discouraged, refers to businessmen and plowmen taking things away from him, but he does not understand what it is that they are stealing. The thief rejoins in a way that is vaguely reassuring yet still elliptical, implying that the two of them share some knowledge of life that sets them apart from others, but that their conversation must cease in light of some mysterious event that is about to happen. The final two couplets suggest that event, with a wildcat's growl, the rising wind, and riders approaching in the distance. The song ends with an air of anticipation, always anxious but never resolved.

Set against acoustic guitar, drums, piano, bass, and some pedal steel guitar, *John Wesley Harding* was a mournful voice in the midst of the volatile late 1960s. In 1978, Dylan said that the record "was a fearful album—just dealing with fear, but dealing with the devil in a fearful way, almost. All I wanted to do was get the words right." Student uprisings across America, as well as in European cities such as Paris and Berlin, expressed the discontent of the young over the older generation's domination of social issues. Young people in the United States looked for heroes, while real ones, such as Martin Luther King, Jr., and Robert Kennedy, were being assassinated. But Dylan had forever relinquished the role of hero for himself, and the quiet traditionalism and spiritual undercurrent of *John Wesley Harding* were his contributions to

the fragmented social scene. Once again many people were surprised, not only by the lyrics but by the musical style that Dylan had chosen to pursue. When *The Basement Tapes* were finally released in 1975, however, they helped people understand that *John Wesley Harding* had not come out of nowhere, and that the songs had evolved during Dylan's long days and deep nights of improvisation with the Band at Big Pink.

In 1967, most people did not know about the tapes, and Dylan had not been seen publicly since prior to his well-documented motorcycle accident. Therefore, in January 1968, when it was announced that Dylan would make his first public appearance in more than two years, the music world felt a wave of curious anticipation. Woody Guthrie, who had exerted such a strong influence in Dylan's life, had died on October 3, 1967. Friends and associates of Guthrie's planned a concert at New York's

Dylan (center) performs with Rick Danko (left) and Robbie Robertson (right) of the Band at the Woody Guthrie Memorial Concert on January 20, 1968, at New York's Carnegie Hall. Singer Odetta, who was one of Dylan's first folk heroes, is seated at the right. The concert was Dylan's first public appearance since his motorcycle accident in July 1966.

Carnegie Hall to honor Guthrie's work, with a program that included a long list of well-known musicians and speakers.

The concert was noteworthy not only because of its honoree but also because its list of accomplished performers included singers such as Arlo Guthrie (Woody's son), Judy Collins, Tom Paxton, Richie Havens, and Pete Seeger. But what transcended this illustrious cast was Dylan's appearance at the concert, his first in 20 months. When he appeared onstage at Carnegie Hall on January 20, 1968, fans saw a heavier Dylan with shorter hair and a bearded face. Backed by the Band, his music was different from the last live music that anyone had heard him perform, as he dove into the country-tinged earthiness that characterized *John Wesley Harding* and the bootleg tapes (*The Basement Tapes*). He performed "Dear Mrs. Roosevelt," "Grand Coulee Dam," and "I Ain't Got No Home." In spite of the newness of the musical sound, fans were delighted to see the man who had been their musical "prophet," and instead of the mixed reception that had greeted his concerts before the motorcycle accident, the audience roared back its approval.

From this auspicious return, Dylan reentered public life. Not long after the Carnegie Hall concert, he and his manager of many years, Albert Grossman, went separate ways. (Dylan managed his own business affairs for some time, while litigation over the terms of settlement continued on even after Grossman's death in 1986.) In February 1969, Dylan went to Nashville, Tennessee, and recorded his next album, *Nashville Skyline,* which was released in April. It, too, took a turn toward country roots. Johnny Cash, a revered singer of country music and a longtime supporter of Dylan and his musical explorations, joined him in "Girl from the North Country." The album was very successful, crossing over from country music to the mainstream pop market. Dylan used a smaller country-music ensemble for his instrumental backup, and the album's songs expressed simple ideas about love and comfortable, immediate relationships. "Lay, Lady, Lay," which became one of Dylan's most popular songs, "To Be Alone with You," and "Tonight I'll Be Staying Here with You" all celebrate spending a night with a lover. Others, like "I Threw It All Away," were about a cherished love that was regrettably lost. As with *John Wesley Harding*, Dylan had taken his lyrics a self-conscious step away from the complexity of his past toward a simpler, clearer persona.

Though Dylan's music had a country feel, he personally began to turn back to the city. Woodstock, since the 1969 Woodstock festival, had become so popularized that it lost much of its reclusive quality. Held during the weekend of August 15–17 on a farm in Bethel, New York, only about 60 miles away from Woodstock, the festival

About a half-million young people camped out at the Woodstock Music and Art Fair during the weekend of August 15–17, 1969. The music festival in upstate New York unified an entire generation for a weekend of experimentation— with psychedelic drugs, uninhibited sexual behavior, and "acid" rock music.

had given birth to what quickly became known as the Woodstock Nation, an image of rebellion against convention, youth against the older generation and "the Establishment." The Woodstock Music and Art Fair attracted about half a million fans, who camped at the farm to listen to the amplified music played by such musicians as Janis Joplin; Jimi Hendrix; the Who; Richie Havens; Melanie; the Incredible String Band; Santana; Joan Baez; Arlo Guthrie; Jefferson Airplane; Blood, Sweat and Tears; the Paul Butterfield Blues Band; Crosby, Stills, Nash & Young; and Sha Na Na, among others. The coming together of the young people—the hippies, the flower children, and the Vietnam War protestors—at Woodstock symbolized the solidarity of a generation.

But Dylan chose not to attend the pop music festival. He decided instead to take his family on a two-week vacation to the Isle of Wight, a small island just off the southern coast of England, where he had been asked to perform. Unfortunately, Dylan underestimated his popularity in Great Britain, and the festival was attended by more than 200,000 fans. After keeping the audience waiting for two hours, the Band played a one-hour set with Dylan, who apparently had been unnerved by the size of the crowd. After he and his family returned to New York, Dylan told reporters that he did not wish to return to England, "They make too much of singers over there," he explained. "Singers are front-page news."

The widespread media focus on Woodstock had become overwhelming for many of the area's residents, particularly the Dylan family, as fans, tourists, and reporters regularly found their way to Dylan's door. By this time, his family included Maria, the daughter from Sara's first marriage whom Dylan adopted, Jesse, and Anna, who was born in the summer of 1967. (Eventually, there would be two more children, Samuel, born in 1969, and

Jakob, born in 1971.) In 1969, Dylan and his family moved from Woodstock back to New York City's Greenwich Village, where Dylan had first begun his career, to a townhouse on MacDougal Street.

But even there he found no solitude. Fans were pleased to see Dylan back in the city. Many were curious about whether or not he was writing new music, a few were still focused on the Dylan of the old days, and one man in particular became obsessed with Dylan's personal life. A. J. Weberman, allegedly a fan of Dylan's, hounded him ruthlessly, waited for him outside his house, went through his garbage for indications of Dylan's home life, and carefully memorized all of Dylan's songs so that he could study them for possible signs of "corruption." Apparently, he was not a fan of the new Dylan, and Weberman, who wrote for underground newspapers, hoped he could try to persuade Dylan to return to the counterculture fold. Weberman, although an extreme personal annoyance to him, represented society's obsession with Dylan as a celebrity.

Back in the bustle of New York City, Dylan gradually became active and creative again. His professional life still progressed at a slower pace than before the accident, but he steadily integrated himself back into the musical scene around him. Unlike most rock stars, Dylan has always appreciated and sought out the company of other musicians, and beginning in the early 1970s, he went to a variety of concerts citywide and invited other singers and musicians into the recording studio with him. He worked

Two hundred thousand fans sing and clap at the Isle of Wight Music Festival on August 31, 1969. Dylan decided to play at the concert in Great Britain instead of the one at Woodstock. His brief performance was controversial; the fans had been mistakenly told that he and the Band would play for more than three hours.

71

with poet and friend Allen Ginsberg and singers Johnny Cash, John Prine, George Harrison, and Eric Clapton, among others.

In 1970, Dylan surprised his audience once again when he released a double album called *Self Portrait,* whose cover was a self-portrait painted by Dylan. (Dylan had begun painting seriously while in Woodstock in 1968–69; one of his works appeared on the cover of the Band's debut album, *Music from Big Pink,* which was released in 1968.) On *Self Portrait,* Dylan played popular songs, such as the standard "Blue Moon" and Paul Simon's "The Boxer." This new twist in Dylan's music making met with great critical disapproval. Earlier albums that had generated surprise or controversy had done so because of Dylan's stylistic changes. But with *Self Portrait,* people thought he had betrayed his artistic standards by doing poor versions of other people's

The Band and Dylan (who is flanked by Rick Danko and Robbie Robertson) perform at the Isle of Wight Music Festival. John Lennon of the Beatles, who attended the concert, said "[Dylan] gave a reasonable, albeit slightly flat, performance, but everyone was expecting Godot, a Jesus, to appear."

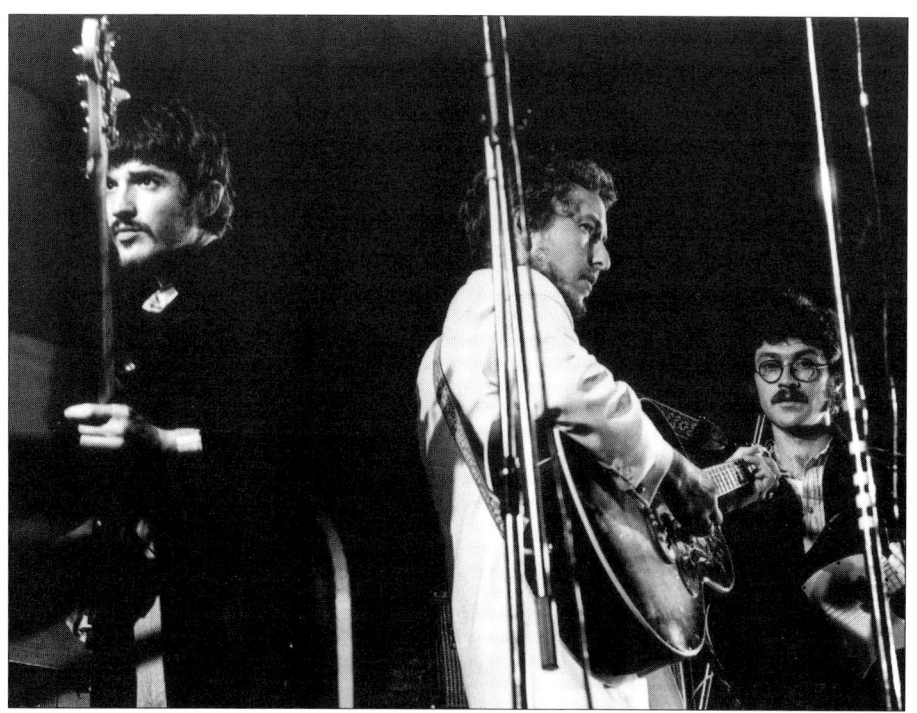

material instead of writing his own. In 1981, Dylan spoke about the reason he put out the album:

> At that time . . . I didn't like the attention I was getting. I [had] never been a person that wanted attention. And at that time I was getting the wrong kind of attention, for doing things I'd never done. So we released the album to get people off my back. They would not like me any more. That's . . . the reason that album was put out, so that people would just at that time stop buying my records, and they did.

With *New Morning,* also released in 1970, Dylan returned to his own songs. Al Kooper, who served as coproducer of the album, said,

> He was writing some songs for a stage play [by Archibald MacLeish], a musical version of *The Devil and Daniel Webster,* so some of these songs were from there. That was pretty much the fulcrum for that album. . . . "Day of the Locusts" came from real life. And "Went to See the Gypsy." Same thing. It was just things that were going on in his life. It's like a diary.

"Day of the Locusts" was an ironic commentary on the honorary doctorate degree in music he had received from Princeton University in June 1970. His acceptance of the degree had been frowned upon by some antiestablishment fans. But in the song's images and musical style, people once more heard something of Dylan's own voice. *Rolling Stone* critic Ralph Gleason wrote his review with the headline "We've Got Dylan Back Again." Other reviewers were just as delighted with *New Morning.*

Dylan also began a more overt exploration of his own spirituality around this time, specifically in terms of the Jewish heritage to which he had paid little attention in the 1960s. In May 1971, he traveled to Israel, and he and Sara spent time in the ancient biblical city of Jerusalem.

There were many rumors about what Dylan was actually feeling and thinking about Judaism, including the report that he might change his name back to Zimmerman. Clinton Heylin mentions in his book on Dylan that after Dylan's father died in June 1968, Dylan became more interested in his Jewish heritage. However, Dylan only acknowledged that it was an ongoing personal exploration, especially about the persecution of Jews throughout history.

In 1971, Dylan's novel, *Tarantula,* was published by Macmillan. Dylan had begun writing the book in the early 1960s. It was a stream-of-consciousness collection of various ideas and images, some of which were clearer than others. A few lines reveal the way that, even in 1966, Dylan had felt about his relationship with the public:

> here lies bob dylan
> demolished by Vienna politeness—
> which will now claim to have invented him
> the cool people can
> now write Fugues about him
> & Cupid can now kick over his kerosene lamp—
> —bob dylan killed by a discarded Oedipus
> who turned
> around
> to investigate a ghost
> & discovered that
> the ghost too
> was more than one person

Another major reappearance came on August 1, 1971, when two benefit concerts were organized by former Beatle George Harrison for the refugees of Bangladesh, whose people were endangered by the warring factions in Pakistan and by drought. When Harrison approached him, Dylan agreed to perform at the Madison Square Garden concerts, his only live appearance in 1971. With his acoustic guitar and harmonica, and with Harrison, former Beatle Ringo Starr, and bassist Leon Russell backing him up, Dylan played some of the old favorites like "Mr. Tambourine Man" and "Blowin' in the Wind," reassuring the jubilant audience that he was still the same Bob Dylan.

In November 1971, he recorded his first song since 1963 that was definitely about a current news event: the murder of African-American writer and activist George Jackson. Jackson was suspiciously killed in a California prison uprising. In response, Dylan quickly wrote "George Jackson" and released it as a single. Though some criticized it as a political move on Dylan's part to get attention and recall his image as an activist, to many others it seemed like an honorable reminder that personal confusion had not altered his sense of morality after all.

In June 1973, most of Dylan's song lyrics, jacket notes, and sketches were put together and published in a book entitled *Writings and Drawings.* The collection was a testament to the poetic body of Dylan's oeuvre, which had drawn attention as *poetry,* not merely as song lyrics. Increasingly, students and professors in colleges and universities looked to Dylan as a subject, sometimes focusing on his lyrics, sometimes studying him in the context of the turbulent 1960s, of which he had become a symbol. In addition to the lyrics of the songs on his albums, the collection also included the lyrics to songs that had not yet been released as recordings. He prefaced the book with four lines, proclaiming:

> If I cant please everybody
> I might as well not please nobody at all
> (but there's so many people
> an I just cant please them all)

These were telling lines from a man who had spent so much of his life contending with other people's expecta-

Dylan (right) makes a surprise appearance after midnight at a New Year's Eve concert in New York on January 1, 1972. Dylan played four songs with the Band (Robbie Robertson is behind Dylan), indicating that he might return to live performances.

tions. *Writings and Drawings* posed only one difficulty. By the 1970s, Dylan had come to regularly alter his songs during live performances. By slightly changing the lyrics, rhythms, and sometimes even melody lines, he would transform a live performance into an unusual new rendering of a song. Sometimes these versions were not as successful as the originals; but sometimes they were extraordinary, paying tribute to Dylan's rich musical inventiveness. The lyrics in the book (published in an updated edition in 1985) could only account for one version of Dylan's lyrics. Many of his changes are traceable only on recordings or have been lost entirely.

One experiment of Dylan's that *was* well documented was his acting in the 1973 Metro-Goldwyn-Mayer

(MGM) Western *Pat Garrett & Billy the Kid.* The movie, directed by Sam Peckinpah, was set in late-19th-century Mexico and filmed on location in Durango, Mexico. Dylan plays Alias, a printer's apprentice who hits the trail with Billy the Kid. Dylan shared the spotlight with the young singer-actor Kris Kristofferson, who stars as Billy the Kid, and the renowned actor James Coburn, who plays Pat Garrett, the outlaw turned lawman who is hired to hunt down his former cohort, Billy. Dylan also applied his musical talents to the film, writing and recording its soundtrack, which featured "Knockin' on Heaven's Door." After MGM removed Peckinpah from the film, it was drastically reedited, and most critics agree that the final version does not live up to Peckinpah's vision.

By the early 1970s, many of Dylan's musician friends had moved away from the East Coast to Los Angeles, California. After their three months in Mexico, Dylan and his family moved to a new home in Malibu, just outside Los Angeles, that he had had built for them. The house, which he called Xanadu, was a huge mansion with a large copper dome. It would offer them some relief from the chaotic New York crowds and fans from whom they were fleeing.

Dylan also made some other changes in his life: though he had recorded exclusively with Columbia Records since his first contract in 1961, he had come to feel that Columbia was no longer interested in him. He signed a short-term contract with David Geffen, an ambitious young man who had begun his own record label called Asylum Records. But Columbia did, in fact, care about what Dylan did and responded to his move with a vengeance by taking old versions of songs he had re-corded—some of his original material, as well as some covers—and releasing them as an album, entitled *Dylan.* These versions had been left over from earlier recording sessions and were renditions that Dylan had chosen not to release on an album. Dylan became even more displeased with Columbia; the company's actions were a sign, not only of how important Dylan was to them, but of just how much power they had over him. In the end, however, the singer grew disenchanted with Asylum and returned to Columbia in September 1974.

During his brief association with Asylum, Dylan did cut two albums for Geffen, *Planet Waves* and *Before the Flood*. For many people, both marked a return to his former creativity, with their rich, eclectic musical style and poetic lyrics. *Planet Waves* harkened back to the deep personal expression of his earlier work, and Dylan and the Band recorded it in just over a week; appearing on the cover was a sketch made by Dylan of three faces, each of which might have been a reflection of him. *Before the Flood* was based on the 1974 concert tour with the Band.

Alias (Dylan) sings a song for some children in MGM's 1973 Western *Pat Garrett & Billy the Kid*. In his commercial movie debut, Dylan plays a printer's assistant who follows Billy the Kid.

This tour had been very successful, as Dylan and the Band reworked many of his old songs into the new concert versions that audiences came to expect. Unlike the audiences of the world tour held before Dylan's motorcycle accident, fans cheered the electric band and welcomed Dylan's mix of old and new songs. The albums and the tour together suggested that Dylan had restored something of his old relationship with his fans.

In general, Dylan wandered through a maze of inconsistent activities during the early 1970s. From benefit concerts to recording sessions, from massive concert tours to a varied set of albums, Dylan seemed to be dodging the legacy of his earlier career while trying to go on with an as-yet-undefined new one. The mid-to-late 1970s, however, were to bring a level of turbulence to his life that ranged from a divorce from Sara and an erratic touring schedule to his conversion to Christianity. For many fans, these changes would irrevocably dispel any notion of a sense of direction in Dylan's career.

Xanadu, the cliffside mansion Dylan had built in Malibu, California, as a retreat for his family, was called a "terrible mismash" architecturally by a county building inspector in 1976. The house cost more than $2 million to construct.

6 Good-byes

DURING THE 1970s, Dylan wandered musically as his politics turned in a milder—or at least a subtler— direction. What had once been exploratory transformations along a single course during the 1960s became, instead, chameleonlike and disconnected changes in the decade that followed. Many people still seemed to be more interested in the past images of Dylan than in the real man. The Dylan of the mid-1960s came to be the point of reference for critics, who compared new rock performers with Dylan's earlier persona. Some young musicians—such as singers Paul Simon, Patti Smith and, in particular, Bruce Springsteen—were referred to as New Dylans. Many artists, young and old, were performing his songs, proving that his music had become a regular part of the rock repertoire. A whole generation of singer-songwriters coming of age in the late 1960s and 1970s were irrevocably touched by Dylan's lyrics. Paul Simon, Jackson Browne, Leonard Cohen, and Van Morrison were all able to be folk-influenced singer-songwriters because Dylan had established the precedent.

On December 8, 1975, the Rolling Thunder Revue performs at a benefit concert for former boxer Rubin "Hurricane" Carter in New York. The entertainers, from left to right, include Roger McGuinn, Joni Mitchell, Richie Havens, Joan Baez, Ramblin' Jack Elliott, and Bob Dylan.

Bootleg recordings of Dylan's performances and studio outtakes—versions done in the recording studio but rejected for the final album—continued to circulate widely, spawning controversy about the ethics of such illegal recordings. Those who were opposed to bootleg recordings felt that they were an infringement on artists' rights, taking away their ability to choose what material they released as their own. But others felt that, especially in the case of an artist like Dylan who gave such varied and inspired performances, it was important to have access to bootleg versions to fully understand an artist's work.

By 1974, Dylan had severe marital difficulties with Sara. He later attributed much of the trouble to a change in his own life that stemmed from art lessons he had taken in March 1974. His friends had told him of an elderly Jewish teacher named Norman Raeben, who gave painting and philosophy lessons. Dylan signed up, and the lessons had a profound impact on him, not only artistically but psychologically as well. Clinton Heylin quotes Dylan's explanation, given in 1978:

Bruce Springsteen was called "The Next Dylan" by Columbia Records, which released Springsteen's first album, *Greetings from Asbury Park, N.J.,* in January 1973. He greatly admired Dylan's talent and had even read a biography of the influential singer-songwriter before John Hammond signed Springsteen up for Columbia.

[Some friends] were talking about truth and love and beauty and all these words I had heard for years and they had 'em all defined. . . . I asked them, "Where do you come up with all those definitions?" and they told me about this teacher. . . . He taught you [about] putting your head and your mind and your eye together. . . . He looked into you and told you what you were. . . . My mind and my hand

and my eye were not connected up. I had a lot of fantasy dreams. . . . Needless to say, it changed me. I went home after that and my wife never did understand me ever since that day. That's when our marriage started breaking up. She never knew what I was talking about, what I was thinking about, and I couldn't possibly explain it.

There has been no public account of Sara's view of the marital problems the couple were having. Whether Dylan's experience with Raeben alone was responsible for their troubles is uncertain. But the couple separated, and in January 1975, Dylan released an album under the Columbia label, inspired by his life with Sara, that was seen by many to be one of his best albums ever.

The pain-filled *Blood on the Tracks* used the rich musical style and poetic language of the albums from the mid-1960s, such as *Blonde on Blonde,* but it used them in examining all the pieces of a broken relationship. The degree to which the songs are truly autobiographical is debatable; Dylan himself claimed that the album was not so much about Sara in any literal sense as it was about his experience of growing apart from her. Though he had recorded *Blood on the Tracks* in only three studio sessions that September in New York, just before its release, he retreated to a studio in Laredo, Minnesota, near Minneapolis, where he had recently bought a farm. There he rerecorded all but three tracks, changing some of the more candid references to his relationship with Sara and crafting the songs into slightly more reserved versions. But in spite of the abstract nature of some of the lyrics, it was clear that the album was a very personal commentary on his own life.

Some of the songs, such as "Tangled Up in Blue" or "Simple Twist of Fate," obviously drew on his and Sara's struggles and on the theme of a deeply established bond between two people who are plagued by the incompatibility of their individual lives. "Simple Twist of

Fate" moodily shifts points of view over the course of the song. The singer at first talks about two lovers as though they were not connected to him in any way, but then he acknowledges that he is singing about himself and that he is part of the tale he is telling. Throughout the song, his view of the couple suggests a sense of destiny, the power and inevitability of their relationship; and that the relationship is dissolved is all part of the "twist of fate."

Not all of the songs attempt to treat both sides of the relationship. "Idiot Wind" is very bitter and forceful, suggesting that the singer is the one who had been mistreated, unfairly blamed despite his best efforts. "If You See Her, Say Hello" is more balanced; the singer acknowledges, despite his painful memories, that he understands his lover's departure and still holds her dear. He sings as if he is talking to another man who might meet her and says that despite his bitter memory, he still respects her and wishes her well.

Altogether, the songs of *Blood on the Tracks* marked another high point in Dylan's songwriting. When English critic Michael Gray of *Let It Rock* reviewed the record, he called it "the most strikingly intelligent album of the seventies." The music was Dylan's own highly expressive style that transcended any particular stylistic label like folk or country. His voice was rough and varied, soft in "When You See Her, Say Hello" and all but screaming in "Idiot Wind." His lyrics were pure poetry, alternating between anger and tenderness but always betraying the depth of feeling that his recent personal ordeal had inspired.

Dylan and Sara briefly reconciled in the spring of 1975. They were seen together in public several times, including at the March benefit concert held in San Francisco for Students Need Athletic and Cultural Kicks (SNACK), in which Dylan performed. But that April,

Dylan traveled to France alone. Once again, the couple's relationship was unclear.

During the summer, Dylan wandered around Greenwich Village, visiting friends, listening to many other musicians, and jamming with blues artist Muddy Waters and singers Patti Smith, Roger McGuinn, and Neil Young. There was such a high level of musical activity around him that Dylan, who had always particularly appreciated the company of other musicians, was suddenly struck with a novel idea: why not take this great musical scene on the road? The Rolling Thunder Revue, as this celebratory musical caravan was called, would help mark America's bicentennial—the 200th anniversary of the signing of the Declaration of Independence—and would provide Dylan with his next major project.

He contacted new and old friends, from Joan Baez and Allen Ginsberg to David Bowie's former guitarist Mick Ronson, and convinced them all to join him on a grand road trip across the country. In October 1975, the newly assembled Rolling Thunder crew kicked off their tour at Gerde's Folk City, Dylan's old haunt from the early 1960s. And in November, the Rolling Thunder Revue hit the road in a bus named Phydeaux (a purposefully awkward spelling of the traditional pet name "Fido"). They played next in Plymouth, Massachusetts, and through the spring of 1976 traveled across the entire country. They rolled from city to city, from state to state, ignoring rock show conventions and creating an uproar in the concert world. By the mid-1970s, it had become routine for rock shows to be held in stadiums and arenas and to be exhaustively and expensively promoted far ahead of time. Dylan's rolling revue, like so much of his life, directly contradicted what, to the music business, had become habit. They did play some large arenas, such as New York City's Madison Square Garden, but they also played in small bars and concert halls, sometimes announced far ahead of time and sometimes just before the show. They might even show up completely unexpected, and only those lucky enough to have decided to go out for a drink that night would hear them.

For the Rolling Thunder Revue performances, Dylan once again threw his audiences a curveball. Rather than walking out in his usual concert attire, he began to use theatrical makeup, often whitening his face and dramatically emphasizing his eyes. Once he even wore a plastic mask. Dylan claimed to have been inspired by the commedia dell'arte (comedy of art), a type of Italian comedy developed in the 16th century in which stock characters improvised using a plot outline. Filmmaker Howard Alk came along on the tour and filmed more than 110 hours of the performances, the bus rides, the parties, and the life backstage. In his biography of Dylan, Clinton Heylin wrote, "The players, both onstage and in the film, were living out their roles to their logical conclusions. The musicians stuck to the same core material, yet every night the show was different, spontaneous and of the moment."

During a period of reconciliation, Dylan's wife, Sara, had come along for some of the tour. Alk's film follows Dylan, Sara, and the other performers, such as Baez and Ginsberg, capturing not only the group's camaraderie, but also Dylan's renewed love affair with Baez, an association that continued to haunt his relationship with his wife. Dylan had a definite idea in mind for the film, which he called *Renaldo and Clara,* and he spent almost a year of his life editing it. The movie revolved around a trio of characters: Renaldo, Clara, and the Woman in White. Allen Ginsberg interpreted the film for Heylin:

> You'd have to study it like *Finnegans Wake,* or Cézanne, to discern the texture, the composition of the tapestry. . . . He put all the scenes on index cards, according to some preconceptions he had when he was directing the shooting. Namely, themes: God, rock and roll, art, poetry, marriage,

women, sex, Bob Dylan, poets, death—maybe eighteen or twenty thematic preoccupations. Then he also put on index cards all the different characters, as well as the scenes. He also marked . . . the dominant color—blue or red . . . and certain other images that go through the movie, like the rose and the hat, and Indians—American Indians. . . . And then he went through it all again and began composing it, thematically . . . the idea was not to have a plot, but to have a composition of those themes. . . . It's a painter's film, and was composed like that.

After the scathing reviews of *Renaldo and Clara* appeared, Dylan found himself defending the film: "The film is no puzzle, it's A-B-C-D, but the composition's like a game—the red flower, the hat, the red and blue themes. The interest is not in the literal plot but in the associated texture—colors, images, sounds." In 1977, Dylan commented further, "The whole movie was his [Renaldo's] dream. . . . Renaldo lives in a tomb, his only way out is to dream." Then a year later, Dylan explained, "The movie creates and holds time. That's what it should do—it should hold that time, breathe in that time and stop time in doing that. It's like if you look at a painting by Cézanne, you get lost in the painting for that period of time. And you breathe—yet time is going by and you wouldn't know it. You're spellbound."

Dylan edited the film down to a four-hour version (and, later, a two-hour version), and it ran in only a few cinemas. The film, however, was not strong as a rock documentary, and critics were largely unsympathetic. Dylan, as usual, did not let the criticism affect his work; however, he reprimanded the negative reporters when he said, "Reading the reviews of the movie, I sensed a feeling of them wanting to crush things. Those reviews weren't about the movie. They were just an excuse to get at me for one reason or another. . . . I was disappointed that the critics couldn't get beyond the superficial elements. They thought the movie was all about Bob Dylan, Joan Baez and Sara Dylan . . . and [it] wasn't."

In the midst of the road trip, Dylan continued to work on his idiosyncratic projects. He became interested in the case of a boxer named Rubin "Hurricane" Carter, who was imprisoned for the 1966 murder of a bartender and two customers in Paterson, New Jersey. Carter's case had been suspicious from the start, and he claimed to have been falsely accused of the killings. Carter had sent Dylan a copy of his autobiography, *The Sixteenth Round.* After reading it, Dylan went to visit Carter in prison in 1975, and they talked for a long time. "The first time I saw him [Carter], I left knowing one thing . . . I realized that the man's philosophy and my philosophy were running on the same road, and you don't meet too many people like that. . . . I took notes because I wasn't aware of all the facts, and I thought that maybe some time I could condense it all down and put it into a song." Dylan wrote "Hurricane" that year and it would appear on his next album, *Desire.*

The Rolling Thunder Revue twice performed a so-called Night of the Hurricane concert, first at Madison Square Garden and then at the Houston Astrodome, to raise money for Carter's defense during his retrial. However, these benefit concerts were not a financial success. Carter was found guilty two more times but was eventually freed on bail in 1985.

Dylan put out *Desire,* another highly successful album, in 1976. He collaborated with songwriter Jacques Levy on the lyrics, and the result was a worthy successor to *Blood on the Tracks.* With the exception of "Hurricane," most of the songs on the album concerned the subject of women. "Isis" refers to the Egyptian goddess and to the mythic image of a hero in search of a treasure, both of which come together in the singer's drive to be with one particular woman. There is something about Isis that

consistently draws the singer back to her but at the same time repels him. He goes on a pilgrimage, searching for an unnamed treasure. When he reaches its site, he finds nothing. The treasure's lure has been deceptive, and he returns to Isis to seek his destiny there. "Oh, Sister" deals with an ambiguous female figure. She could be a familial sister or a metaphorical "sister" who is really a lover, from whom Dylan asks acceptance and compassion. The song "Sara" was inspired by his wife and is threaded with autobiographical references, not in the angry, volatile way of "Blood on the Tracks," but in a way that is gently self-revealing: he remembers sitting up in the Chelsea Hotel writing "Sad-Eyed Lady of the Lowlands" for her.

By the mid-1970s, the members of the Band, despite their success in performing behind Dylan and on their own, had come to feel that it was time to go in separate directions. They announced that their final concert

In January 1976, Dylan and Bobby Neuwirth perform at Houston's Astrodome to help raise money for Rubin "Hurricane" Carter's defense. Dylan premiered much of his new material with the Rolling Thunder Revue and enjoyed a special bond that formed among the musicians.

would be held in November 1976 at the Winterland theater in San Francisco, and they invited many of their friends to join them, including Dylan. Singers ranging from Emmylou Harris and Joni Mitchell to Muddy Waters and Van Morrison all came onstage with them, in an unusual and creative moment in rock history. That moment was captured on film as well. Robbie Robertson was a close friend of the young filmmaker Martin Scorsese. In what has become one of the most outstanding examples of rock documentary, Scorsese borrowed lights, cameras, and sets from the local opera company and filmed the Band's final concert celebration. The resulting movie, called *The Last Waltz,* captures the remarkable music making, the camaraderie, and the communication among the Band and their guests.

The film also reveals how Dylan, with no particular effort to do so, became the focus of the event when he

In November 1976, Dylan sings with the Band during the Band's final live performance in San Francisco, California. The spectacular concert was recorded by filmmaker Martin Scorsese and the resulting movie, *The Last Waltz,* is considered by most to be one of the best rock documentaries ever made.

performed with the Band. Together, they played a hard-driving, rhythmic version of "Baby Let Me Follow You Down," a lyrical diversion that included "I Don't Believe You" and "Forever Young," and then a return to "Follow You Down." The Band then joined Dylan in "I Shall Be Released," one of the songs from their days at Big Pink. The song was a hymnlike meditation on some unspecified confinement or constraint, and the belief that liberation would come. It was almost spiritual in its calm yearning, its meditative distance on a life being lived, and its fervent belief in change. For Dylan, it was a poignant musical tribute to a group of musicians who had been a very important part of his life. It was typical of his enigmatic character to close with a song that looked beyond the moment to something larger and inexplicable, putting a mystical frame around the event.

But there were still more good-byes to be said. Dylan's problems with his wife came to a head in February 1977, when he and Sara irrevocably separated. In her own account, Sara claimed to have come downstairs and found another woman at the breakfast table with Dylan and the children. Dylan allegedly hit Sara in the face and asked her to leave. She filed for divorce, citing domestic violence as one of her grievances. The divorce hearings continued through the summer and into the fall (while Dylan was involved in editing *Renaldo and Clara*), including a rather ugly custody battle, and the legal matters were finally resolved in November.

In the wake of the divorce, Dylan pressed on with his live concerts, which, despite his periodic albums, were fast becoming the focus of his professional life. In 1978, he ventured his biggest world tour yet, traveling to Japan, Australia, England, and West Germany (now part of Germany). It was the first time that people in Europe or the Far East had been able to see Dylan tour since his motorcycle accident, and they were wildly enthusiastic.

Because the Band had broken up, Dylan assembled an unusually large backup band made up of friends who were also top-notch musicians. He also decided to do many of his old songs along with the more recent ones, but he chose to present them in a new form, slightly altering the lyrics, melodic lines, and rhythms and giving the audiences the songs that they loved in a fresh way. The concerts in Europe and the Far East were very successful financially and reestablished Dylan's preeminence as a rock star, even as punk and disco music rose to the fore in pop culture. Artists such as the Sex Pistols and Elvis Costello reinvented the original brashness and social iconoclasm of early rock and roll, and disco music, with its emphasis on dance and electronically produced rhythms, was widely popular. But Dylan remained largely untouched by either style.

In June 1978, he released *Street-Legal,* which was well liked by fans, and in July *Bob Dylan at Budokan,* recorded at a concert in Tokyo, Japan. In September he finished the European tour, for which he received favorable reviews, and immediately began touring in the United States. Dylan was keeping up a rigorous and exhausting pace, playing between 10 and 20 concerts per month. The nights were long and the days were hard. Many writers criticized Dylan's American concerts and panned recent albums as well as the film *Renaldo and Clara.* Dylan was worn out, ragged, disappointed, and alone.

At a concert in San Diego, California, while struggling through a long set, someone threw a silver crucifix onto the stage. Dylan later recalled the incident:

> Usually I don't pick things up in front of the stage. . . . But I looked down at that cross. I said, "I gotta pick that up." So I picked up the cross and I put it in my pocket. . . . And I brought it backstage and I brought it with me to the next town, which was out in Arizona. . . . I was feeling even worse than I'd felt when I was in San Diego. I said, "Well,

During his world tour in 1978, Dylan performs before a crowd in St. Paul, Minnesota, on Halloween. Dylan had been traveling nonstop for months and was angry at the American critics, who, unlike the Australian, Japanese, and European reporters, reviewed his concerts unfavorably.

I need something tonight." I didn't know what it was. I was used to all kinds of things. I said, "I need something tonight that I didn't have before." And I looked in my pocket and I had this cross.

In the Arizona hotel room that night, Dylan had an experience that he described as being "born again," an experience that would inspire his life—his lyrics, his music, and his philosophy—for the next two years.

7 ★ Changes

IN 1979, DYLAN SHOCKED THE WORLD with yet another unanticipated transformation. The 1960s radical and social activist now turned to an overt, all-consuming, and frequently judgmental brand of Christianity called the Vineyard School of Discipleship. Many of his fans were unable to follow him on this particular course. Mary Alice Artes, his girlfriend at the time, shared his religious conviction and encouraged Dylan to explore it. About his conversion, Dylan said simply that "Jesus put his hand on me. It was a physical thing. I felt my whole body tremble. The glory of the Lord knocked me down and picked me up."

Dylan's conversion became wholly reflected in his music, as he began to produce songs that expressed and explored his spiritual experiences. The first album to be written under the influence of his newfound Christianity was *Slow Train Coming,* released on August 18, 1979. It was produced by Jerry Wexler, the producer for Atlantic Records who had also made albums for such remarkable singers as Aretha Franklin and Ray Charles. On *Slow Train Coming,* Dylan's songs ranged in musical style, but each one centered on the

Dylan sings in Oslo, Norway, in 1981. After his conversion to Christianity, Dylan remarked about his religious songs, "I was saying stuff I figured people needed to know. I thought I was giving people an idea of what was behind the songs."

theme of Christian belief as the only path to truth. "I Believe in You" is a quiet, impassioned song that is somewhat abstract in its images. It could be understood as belief in a deity or as an unusual love song. The singer vows his belief in his beloved through a full range of experiences: tears as well as laughter; the morning after the night spent together; the lack of acceptance by others. "When He Returns" deals with more concrete images. Over a gospel-style piano accompaniment, Dylan sings about Christ's Second Coming. The lyrics encourage the listener to admit a fundamental humanity, the weaknesses of which could never be truly hidden from God, and to surrender to a larger divine plan.

The sense of moral judgment in these songs (for example, in the line "How long can you falsify and deny what is real?") is set into what was for Dylan a new context of Christian ideas, but it was not entirely uncharacteristic of him. Early songs like "The Death of Emmett Till" or "The Lonesome Death of Hattie Carroll" were also strong statements about right and wrong. *John Wesley Harding* had had the air of a spiritual search. Events that come from the Bible had often appeared in Dylan's lyrics, including Christ's crucifixion in "Long Ago, Far Away" and Adam and Eve's Garden of Eden in "Gates of Eden." Even the images of angels, saints, and martyrs, all originally religious ideas, are scattered throughout Dylan's songs. But the difference this time was that they were not simply passing references in otherwise nonreligious lyrics but part of a distinct Christian message. This time, there was nothing ambiguous about Dylan's poetry.

Some songs on *Slow Train Coming* even showed an intolerance for those who might not have embraced Christianity. Some people were offended by such narrow-mindedness, yet it had appeared before in Dylan's music. The early song "Masters of War" was bitterly critical of people who manufactured guns. In the final verse, the singer wishes for the death of the person he sings about and prefaces that wish by saying that, despite his own youth, he is sure that even Christ would not forgive these "masters of war."

Yet if such intolerance had existed in some of Dylan's older lyrics, it had been part of a broader philosophy of caring and compassion for all kinds of people. He criticized arms builders because of what he saw to be the injustice of war. His moral judgment had traditionally been directed only at those who actually endangered or discriminated against others. But in the new lyrics, his point of view was seen as prejudice against anyone who was not a devout Christian. The world suddenly seemed more starkly black and white. Commenting on the album in 1984, Dylan said,

> The songs that I wrote for the "Slow Train" album [frightened me]. . . . I didn't plan to write them, but I wrote them anyway. I didn't like writing them. . . . But I found myself writing these songs and after I had a certain amount of them I thought I didn't want to sing them, so I had a girl sing them for me . . . A girl I was singing with at the time, Carolyn Dennis. . . . I wanted the songs out but I didn't want to do it [myself] because I knew that it wouldn't be perceived in that way. It would just mean more pressure. I just did not want to write at that time.

Critic Jann Wenner of *Rolling Stone* magazine wrote a glowing review of the album, saying that "Musically, this is probably Dylan's finest record, a rare coming together of inspiration, desire and talent that completely fuses strength, vision and art. Bob Dylan is the greatest singer of our times. . . . More than his ability with words, and more than his insight, his voice is God's greatest gift to him."

In October 1979, Dylan appeared on the television show "Saturday Night Live," performing three of his new songs based on his Christian conversion. It was typically ironic for Dylan to play Christian songs in the context of one of the most popular comedy shows in television's history. Many saw the act as audacious in light of his plummeting popularity.

In November, Dylan performed for 14 nights in San Francisco. At these concerts he played only new songs, which was highly unusual for a rock star who had amassed as many hits as Dylan had. Audiences were used to hearing the songs they loved, and they were confused by his new direction. During later concerts, Dylan would often proselytize, an approach that ran counter to the typical performance of a rock star. Yet it was ironic that the same people who had once fully believed every word he said would now not accept his firmest convictions. At one concert in Omaha, Nebraska, Dylan stepped up to the microphone and told the audience, "Years ago they used to say I was a prophet. I'd say, 'No, I'm not a prophet.' They'd say, 'Yes, you are a prophet.' Now I come out and say, 'Jesus is the answer.' They say, 'Bob Dylan? He's no prophet.' They just can't handle that."

Such sermonizing made some people uncomfortable and angry. Around 1980, there had been an increase in the size and power of conservative religious groups in America, a rise that was closely associated with the success of the new Republican president, Ronald Reagan. This conservative movement was often characterized by intolerance of anyone who did not share fundamentalist beliefs—that is, faith in a literal interpretation of the Bible—and it affected a wide range of political issues from a woman's right to have an abortion to programs of social reform. To many of Dylan's old supporters, his new religious proclamations could dangerously be misunderstood as support of such social intolerance. Though Dylan himself might not have shared the social views of the far right, his Christian conviction might be used by those who did.

★ CHANGES ★

In February 1980, Dylan won a Grammy award for Best Male Rock Vocal Performance for his religious song, "Gotta Serve Somebody." After thanking the audience, he went on to say that his Christian songs were as much a part of his music as any of his other songs, and that they could not be separated from his work. In June 1980, he released another religious album entitled *Saved,* which to many was even less effective than *Slow Train Coming.*

On February 27, 1980, Dylan, dressed in a tuxedo, performs "Gotta Serve Somebody," the song for which he was awarded that year's Grammy for Best Male Rock Vocal Performance.

To these critics, Dylan had abandoned his artful sense of poetry, his compassionate social views, and his rich musical gift. Reviewers felt that if he wanted to write religious songs, he should have drawn much more on gospel, a rich and rhythmic musical style that uses biblical sentiments and stories. Yet whatever critics or audiences thought of the music, Dylan's time of Christian faith was still another remarkable sign of his determination to follow his own instincts. That it was not popular for a rock star to publicize or even experience a spiritual revelation was irrelevant to Dylan.

By late 1980, Dylan's songs gradually began to be less and less about Christian zeal and spiritual experience. He again gave performances that included many of his old songs and invited some of his former associates, like Roger McGuinn and Jerry Garcia, to join him in concert. Many fans felt hopeful relief at the sign of a somewhat more familiar Dylan.

He toured extensively throughout the spring and fall of 1981, mainly through Europe, Canada, and the American Midwest, and released another album called *Shot of Love*. It drew on the Christian ideals and images that were still a part of Dylan's life but integrated them with a little of the old Dylan: more tolerance and flexibility, set into the context of general philosophical musings. One of the songs on the album, "Every Grain of Sand," is considered by many to be among the simplest and most beautiful that Dylan has ever written. Its lyrics move through a series of images, which in their evocative, poetic quality, are more typical of Dylan's old work. He alludes to the range of life's experiences, from wonder to utter loneliness and from grief to revelation. Sometimes he feels company close by, either spiritual or human, and sometimes he senses only himself. But he formulates this range with the idea that it is part of a larger plan, an artistic design of life, death, joy, and

woe that, though it spans the ages, can be seen in a single gesture of nature—a falling sparrow or a grain of sand. The sum of life's experiences hang in a balance, the rightness of which must be lived out, if not always understood.

Throughout the tours, Dylan maintained his tradition of altering his songs in live performances. More than most other pop artists, he continued to explore the possibilities inherent in his own material. The results were unpredictable. Some of those variations occasionally ended up being less successful musically, especially during the 1980s, weakening the original song. But sometimes they were inspired changes. When Dylan would sing, he would remold phrases, aware of every syllable. Sometimes, he would alter the rhythmic design

In late September 1983, Dylan (far left) participates in the bar mitzvah ceremony of his son Jakob (far right) at the Wailing Wall in Jerusalem. Speaking in New York in 1983, Dylan said, "That [born-again period] was all part of my experience. It had to happen. When I get involved in something, I get totally involved. I don't just play around on the fringes."

of a line, as in versions of "Lay, Lady, Lay" and "I Threw It All Away," where the concert versions on the live album *Hard Rain* were very different from the original tracks on *Nashville Skyline.* His backup band might play different bass lines or sing different harmony. Now and then, Dylan would even alter the lyrics of a well-known song. These concert variations, however, only fueled the ongoing life of a heavy underground market of bootleg record-

In May 1984, Dylan undertook another world tour and is seen here performing in Hamburg, West Germany (now part of Germany). It had been almost a year since his last recording session (for *Infidels*), and Dylan experimented with new compositions while on tour before beginning to record *Empire Burlesque* in New York in July.

ings. Tapes of Dylan's concerts were valuable as a chronicle of his artistic explorations.

Speculation about Dylan's spiritual inclinations still lingered among both his fans and his critics. Some rumors had him spending time with conservative Jews, while others saw him retaining an interest in Christianity. To many fans, he simply seemed to flounder in undefined experimentation. In the fall of 1983, Dylan visited the Wailing Wall in Jerusalem for the bar mitzvah (the ceremony recognizing a Jewish boy's 13th birthday, at which time he attains the age of religious responsibility) of his son Jakob, an event captured in a much-publicized photograph. He was seen wearing a yarmulke and prayer shawl, a gesture that not only suggested his active participation in the bar mitzvah ceremony, but also the possibility of a self-conscious reconsideration of Judaism for himself.

Dylan's next album, *Infidels,* was further proof that Dylan had left behind a blatant Christianity, though many people—particularly those who had a vested interest in interpreting Dylan one way or the other—still tried to read messages into the lyrics about Dylan's spiritual direction. Released in November 1983, *Infidels* spanned a wide range of styles, with some songs, such as the opening "Jokerman," coming across as stronger than others. But even more important than the songs that were included on the album were those that had been left off. During the recording sessions, Dylan and his musicians had played around with several different tunes. In deciding which ones would go onto the actual release, Dylan had arbitrarily chosen some over others. Some that he rejected at the time, like "Blind Willie McTell," were released on later collections and were so successful, and so well performed, that many people never understood why Dylan had not included them on the original album.

In 1984, Dylan undertook yet another tour, attempting to regain some of the success of his last tour in 1981. He traveled through Europe, including Germany, Spain, France, and the Netherlands. Tickets for his concerts sold slowly, but eventually all of them did sell. His fans were receptive and enthusiastic, many of them being as young as 20 years old. It was clear that even those who had come to know Dylan's music retrospectively liked it just as much as those who had first heard it in the 1960s.

Yet his place in popular music in general had become less clear. Singer Bruce Springsteen (also discovered by John Hammond, the Columbia executive who had first signed Dylan) had become the premiere performer of live rock shows; Michael Jackson and his album *Thriller,* which is perhaps the most popular ever to have been released, and the new Irish band U2 dominated the scene. As Dylan doggedly pursued his tours and personalized albums, a gap appeared between him and other top artists in the pop music world—the disparity of commercial success. Dylan may have been a cornerstone of rock—U2's lead singer, Bono, publicly acknowledged Dylan's influence on the band—but Dylan never achieved the huge record sales of the new megastars of the 1980s like Jackson, U2, or Whitney Houston. Individual songs of Dylan's tended to sell very well as singles, such as "Like a Rolling Stone" or "Lay, Lady, Lay." Yet no album ever had the singular commercial impact of one like Jackson's *Thriller.*

But if Dylan's exact place amid the rising 1980s megastars seemed undefined, there was no question about his place in rock history. The tides of popular music might have surged ahead, leaving Dylan more and more a part of his own idiosyncratic tradition, but there was also an increasing attention to the legend of Bob Dylan. Dylan had contributed to the definition of rock music, and musicians began to refer back to that fact, either humorously or in the context of a serious search for their own artistic identities. During July 1982, the first annual Bob Dylan imitators' contest had been held in Greenwich Village, a comic tribute to the fact that his idiosyncratic style had become an image distinct from its originator. And Dylan's life as a singer-songwriter, following his own path and believing in his own causes, had become a paradigm that young artists looked up to in earnest. By the late 1980s, the presence of superstars had become overwhelming. A few singers, such as Tracy Chapman, Suzanne Vega, and Billy Bragg, began to return to simpler roots, often specifically those of folk music. Bands like the Athens, Georgia–based R.E.M. sought a less inflated musical style and simpler image, one that was truer to their backgrounds and, indeed, their humanity. Dylan had already carved out that prospect.

The high esteem in which most people held Dylan only continued to grow. His current musical activities became secondary to the fact that he had already been a driving force in rock, and it was that legacy of which people were most aware.

8 ⋆ Celebration

DURING THE MID-TO-LATE 1980s, Dylan used his powerful public image in a way that was new but yet also old: to benefit social causes. Because of the severe world crises at the time—plights such as famine and disease— rock musicians offered their craft to help raise money for and awareness of these emergencies, and Dylan's participation in the benefits once again made him highly visible to the public. During late 1984 and throughout 1985, one of the most ravaging famines in recent history occurred. In northeastern Africa, people of all ages began dying in huge numbers. As pictures of starving children—many mere skeletons—appeared in magazines like *Life,* people around the world took action.

In January 1985, a remarkable array of singers—including Diana Ross, Bruce Springsteen, Stevie Wonder, Tina Turner, Michael Jackson, Ray Charles, and Dylan—assembled to record the song and video entitled "We Are the World." The event had received much publicity and, despite the collective concerts of the late 1960s, was novel after the narcissism and conservative politics of the early 1980s. At the recording session, Dylan—

Sharing the billing with Tom Petty and the Heartbreakers before a packed house in Tacoma, Washington, on July 31, 1986, Dylan plays some of his hits from the 1960s.

frequently at odds with the music business—seemed to be less comfortable performing than the others were. It was harder for him to join in with the general spirit of gaiety and celebrity. When he had trouble delivering his line of the song, Stevie Wonder began joking with Dylan, imitating him at the keyboard, hoping to calm him. Dylan soon loosened up and was able to sing his solo. The recording and the video both went to the top of the pop music charts and helped bring in much-needed aid to the starving Ethiopians and others.

On January 28, 1985, Dylan joins a star-studded chorus in recording "We Are the World" for the USA for Africa benefit. Initially, Dylan was uncomfortable during the performance, but with help from Stevie Wonder he soon fell into the genial mood of the gathering.

An even larger benefit effort took place in July 1985. It was a live rock show, called Live Aid, and it reached what was supposedly one of the largest television audiences ever on record, an estimated 2 billion viewers. The show took place in two different stadiums, one in Philadelphia and the other in London, England, and lasted for 16 hours. Artists such as U2, Sting, Tina Turner, and Mick Jagger gave stunning performances in America. Dylan was the closing act, accompanied by two other

guitarists, Keith Richards and Ron Wood, both from the Rolling Stones. All three played acoustic guitars, resulting in a muddy sound, and the effect was not nearly as clear or powerful as the preceding acts. Dylan later said that the stage monitors had been turned off, and he could not hear a thing other than the singers practicing the finale behind the curtain. Dylan began the act with "Ballad of Hollis Brown," and the trio played "When the Ship Comes In" and "Blowin' in the Wind." Dylan went on to make a controversial comment and plea. He noted that U.S. farmers were also having severe troubles while the country was sending American money halfway around the world. Would it be possible, he asked, for some of the money to go to them?

Those who had planned the African famine relief effort were upset by Dylan's request and felt that their cause was not being fully supported. But Dylan's comments, though ill-timed, were the truth, and they fell on receptive ears. Farm Aid was soon organized by Willie Nelson, John Cougar Mellencamp, and Neil Young to raise money for American farmers, and in September 1985, the 14-hour concert was staged at the University of Illinois. Dylan, who was asked to appear at the event, performed with Tom Petty and the Heartbreakers (the musicians he had used on *Shot of Love* and *Empire Burlesque*). The group rehearsed a week before the benefit concert and made sure that the sound checks were run through properly before they were to perform. Most people found Dylan's performance superb and his renditions of "I'll Remember You," "Trust Yourself," "That Lucky Old Sun," and "Maggie's Farm" awe inspiring.

Later that month, he sang on yet another benefit record called *Sun City*. It was put together by "Artists United Against Apartheid," and it helped raise awareness of South Africa's oppressive and discriminatory government.

In July 1985, Ron Wood (left), Dylan, and Keith Richards (right) perform at Live Aid in Philadelphia, Pennsylvania. After his set, Dylan asked the audience whether some of the money raised at the concert could be given to help American farmers who were struggling with their own crisis.

Rock had once more become a distinct vehicle for social change, though in a much different way than it had been in the 1960s. With the 1980s benefits, rock was sanctioned by the mainstream and was an applauded act of social action. In the 1960s, it had been counterculture, often defined as being *against* the mainstream. Nevertheless, a historical connection between the two decades was made when Joan Baez walked onstage at Live Aid and said "This is your Woodstock!" The benefit concerts of the 1980s brought together a myriad of otherwise incongruous artists, such as Dylan, Diana Ross, and U2. Seeing their favorite singers performing together pleased the record buyers. Moreover, because many of the charities involved crises in Third World countries like Ethiopia, or abominable political and social conditions such as those in the black townships of South Africa, the benefits increased Western awareness of the plight of these countries and of their cultures as well. It was during the 1980s that world music became a real presence, with African and Caribbean-influenced styles growing increasingly popular. Dylan's spirit often pervaded the benefits. (On the 1988 Amnesty International Conspiracy of Hope Tour, at which artists banded together to support political victims around the world, Bruce Springsteen would close the show by bringing all the participating musicians onstage for "Chimes of Freedom," powerfully evoking Dylan's essence, even though Dylan himself was not there.) In the midst of all the 1980s benefits, Dylan was never righteous about the causes or self-glorifying about his involvement with them. He gave what he could— sometimes imperfect and unpolished—and diligently avoided the limelight.

Dylan's next album, *Empire Burlesque,* came out in 1985 and was well liked by both fans and critics. Many thought it was the best Dylan album of the 1980s, and it made clear that the judgmental tone of the religious albums had faded. The record expressed an odd range of emotions, many of which seemed tied to wistful memories of one or several former lovers. "I'll Remember You" is a sweet, poignant tribute to a woman he had tried hard to love and support. Though he might not have succeeded with his love in the way she might have wished, he would always remember her as someone who understood him, who saw straight to his core, more than anyone else could. "When the Night Comes Falling from the Sky" is a wild, loose song that expresses both fury and fear over difficulties with a lover, referring back to some final moment—an apocalypse—when everything is confronted and accounted for. He has been away on some journey of his own. She burns his letters yet smiles when she sees him coming back. They have fought over issues that seem intelligible but now have only to do with struggle for struggle's sake. Yet, as in most of Dylan's other arresting love songs, the lovers' pain is underlined by a sense of destiny, that they will find each other again "when the night comes falling from the sky."

With the release of *Empire Burlesque,* Dylan began to investigate the world of music videos, which by this point had gained much in popularity, influence, and prestige. MTV played a crucial part in the way popular music was disseminated, and the opening sequence in Dylan's 1966 film *Don't Look Back,* by uniting a song with footage of the artist interpreting the song rather than just perform-ing it, had been an early stage in the development of the music video. By 1985, Dylan was ready to try and make another music video. He asked filmmaker Paul Schrader to direct the piece, and the two quickly shot a video using "Tight Connection to My Heart." Dylan had been im-pressed with Schrader's movie *Mishima* and agreed to have the video filmed in April in Tokyo, Japan. But Schrader and Dylan did not work well together and quickly rejected the video as a failure. Then in August 1985, with Dave Stewart of the rock group the Euryth-mics, Dylan made two more videos, using *Empire Bur-lesque* songs "When the Night Comes Falling from the Sky" and "Emotionally Yours." Shot in Los Angeles, these videos also failed to achieve the dramatic effect that Dylan had been seeking, and the black-and-white videos had little impact on the MTV viewers. Popular video is apparently one medium for which Dylan has little affinity.

In December 1985, *Biograph,* a summary of Dylan's work, was released. Dylan uncharacteristically granted many revealing interviews around the time of the five-album set's release, and it sold well. *Biograph* was in many ways an unusually accurate portrait of Dylan. Compiled by Jeff Rosen, who worked for Special Rider, Dylan's publishing company, it contained concert performances and studio outtakes (versions of songs that were rejected for the final album), as well as some of his greatest hits in their original form. But in revealing every phase of Dylan's career, *Biograph* also realistically represented many of the highs and lows of Dylan's music, with the inclusion of some performances that were strong, such as a live acoustic rendition of "Visions of Johanna," and some that were weak, such as "Million Dollar Bash" or "Can You Please Crawl Out Your Window?" Also important in the *Biograph* release were the liner notes written by rock critic and screenwriter Cameron Crowe. Crowe, who had long followed Dylan's career and had a deep understanding of his music, interviewed Dylan extensively. Like the collection of songs, Crowe's 32-page notes reveal Dylan's expansive range. Dylan talks about his fears of consumerism and about the way in which rock had become compromised in its association with the commercial world. He also contradicted various rumors that had floated around for years about the meanings of some of his songs.

Also in December 1985, Dylan's lyrics and sketches, originally gathered in the 1973 collection entitled *Writings and Drawings,* were published in an expanded format that included his lyrics to date, as well as album liner notes that Dylan himself had written. *Lyrics 1962–1985,* as the publication was called, *Biograph,* and *Empire Burlesque* contributed significantly to celebrating Dylan's lifetime contribution to the world of music. The public and his own colleagues recognized his artistic legacy with his admission into the Songwriters Hall of Fame in New York City in March 1982 and the presentation to Dylan by the American Society of Composers, Publishers, and

Authors (ASCAP) in March 1986 of their prestigious
Founders Award for his lifetime of valuable work in the
field of popular music.

Some of Dylan's projects during this period had
mixed results. In 1986, he took a principal role in the
film *Hearts of Fire,* directed by Richard Marquand,
who had just completed work on *Jagged Edge.* In *Hearts
of Fire,* Dylan acted the role of a bitter and aging rock
star. But his costars Rupert Everett and Fiona Flanagan
gave weak performances, and the film was poorly received. Iain Smith, line producer of the film, commenting on Dylan's acting in the movie, said, "I think he's
arguably the best thing in the film. . . . He's funny and
quirky and strange and you watch him on the screen and
you think, 'Well, he's not acting. . . , but, and it's a bit
odd, he's very very watchable.' You just want to watch
him. And it's a totally undefinable quality." The film
was briefly shown in England but was never released in
U.S. movie theaters, and it was not until the spring of
1990 that it became available on video.

During the late 1980s, Dylan's concert performances
became more haggard and irregular. There were a few
bright spots, but often his singing was unintelligible, with
years of smoking having taken their toll on his voice. He
sometimes seemed apathetic and uninspired and, in interviews, became not simply evasive but curmudgeonly.
His album *Down in the Groove* (June 1988), on which
other artists such as the Grateful Dead and Eric Clapton
had joined him, sounded haphazard and careless in com-
parison to previous albums.

Yet public esteem for Dylan did not falter, based, as it
was, on the past more than on the present. During a
decade when his fluctuations had been especially inconsistent and, to some critics, ineffective, the legend of
Dylan continued to have a momentum of its own. In
January 1988, when Bruce Springsteen spoke during

Dylan's induction into the Rock and Roll Hall of Fame, he referred to "Like a Rolling Stone," saying,

> Dylan was a revolutionary. Bob freed your mind the way Elvis freed your body. He showed us that just because the music was innately physical did not mean that it was anti-intellectual. He had the vision and the talent to make a pop song that contained the whole world. He invented a new way a pop singer could sound, broke through the limitations of what a recording artist could achieve and changed the face of rock and roll for ever and ever.

In April 1988, Dylan got together with a few of his oldest friends—George Harrison, Roy Orbison, Tom Petty, and Jeff Lynne. They dubbed themselves the Traveling Wilburys and took on fictional names like "Otis" and "Lucky" Wilbury (Dylan). They played music together in Dylan's garage studio in Malibu and

After their induction into the Rock and Roll Hall of Fame on January 20, 1988, George Harrison (left) and Bob Dylan get together for a jam session.

came up with a record, called *Traveling Wilburys,* that was fresh and spontaneous (having been put together in only a few days). Many of the songs (such as "Dirty World," "Congratulations," "Margarita," and "Tweeter and the Monkey Man") were performed in the styles of country and rockabilly music. According to Clinton Heylin, it was Dylan's first platinum album of the eighties, his only double-platinum album ever, and a great commercial success. Sadly, Roy Orbison ("Lefty" Wilbury) died later that year, but the Wilburys, minus one, went on to make a second album in 1990.

Despite these interludes of recording or playing with friends, Dylan never stopped being on the road. In 1988, he began what in his own words was a never-ending tour:

> It's all the same tour. The Never-Ending Tour. . . . It works out better for me that way. You can pick and choose better when you're just out there all the time and your show is already set up. You know, you just don't have to start it up and end it. It's better just to keep it out there with breaks . . . extended breaks.

In September 1989, Dylan released another album, *Oh Mercy,* that was far more cogent and articulate than much of his recent work had been. He hired Daniel Lanois to produce it; Lanois, who is a talented musician, had gained much valuable experience working with artists like U2, Peter Gabriel, and Robbie Robertson. Together, Dylan and Lanois created an album of songs that recaptured Dylan's sense of poetry and personal insight, without any sermonizing, and once again showcased Dylan's rare melodic gift. For example, "The Man in the Long Black Coat" is an eerie allegory in Dylan's former narrative style. And "Most of the Time" is a mystical, rhythmic meditation on the idea that one woman would never quite leave his thoughts. His life goes on, and he is able to deal with whatever comes his way—"most of the time."

Only now and then does her image make him pause. Though dwelling in the past, she is never really gone.

On January 20, 1990, France's minister of culture awarded the Commandeur des Arts et des Lettres, a special honor, to Dylan; he recorded *Under the Red Sky* between January and March 1990, which included such songs as "Wiggle Wiggle," "Under the Red Sky," "Unbelievable," "Born in Time," "T.V. Talkin' Song," and "Cat's in the Well;" and at the 1991 Grammy Awards,

Dylan sings "Masters of War" at the Grammy Awards ceremony in 1991. Actor Jack Nicholson presented Dylan with the Lifetime Achievement Award at the thirty-third annual ceremony.

Dylan received a Lifetime Achievement Award. At the Grammy ceremony, he performed his song "Masters of War." But his delivery was slurred and unclear, obscuring any possible relevance to the Persian Gulf War that was being fought between Iraq and the United Nations' Coalition forces, and his brief speech left the audience baffled. Looking out from the stage, perhaps searching for his mother, he talked about his father being a simple man and about how he never said very much, but one thing that he said was "it is possible to be so defiled in this world that even your mother and father won't know you. But God will always trust in your own abilities to mend your own ways."

In 1991, yet another substantial retrospective of Dylan's work was released, one that finally addressed the bootleg tapes that had been such a salient part of Dylan's legacy. The *Bootleg Series* (three albums in one set) made available, in an official and legal format, many of the recordings that had been circulating on the bootleg black market for years and that had been inaccessible to the general public. With other performers, the unattainability of an artist's work might have been less consequential, but with Dylan, whose brilliance was idiosyncratic and often whimsically expressed, it would never have been possible to evaluate an entire career without the bootleg recordings.

The *Bootleg Series* includes songs from the early 1960s to the late 1980s. There are studio outtakes, where Dylan can be heard laughing or making comments. There are original demos, such as that for "Every Grain of Sand." "Blind Willie McTell," a particularly evocative song that had been recorded during the *Infidels* sessions but rejected for use on that album, is finally incorporated here. There are alternate performances of well-known songs, like "If You See Her, Say Hello" and "Idiot Wind." The versions recorded on the *Bootleg Series* are considered by most critics to be superb examples of Dylan's songwriting abilities and of his most inspired presentations.

In 1992, Dylan turned 50 years old, an event that drew much attention from the media. Bob Dylan, who as a youth had been a symbol of a changing nation and who had inspired a generation both musically and socially, was a half-century old. The birthday celebration (and the 30th anniversary of his first album) was a striking demonstration of the passing of an era, and it posed the question as to what impact the youth who came of age during the 1960s really had on the world's situation today.

The Dylanfest that was held at Madison Square Garden in October 1992 played out the themes that had cropped up throughout Dylan's life: the vast array of musicians who continue to look up to him, the ongoing relevance of his music and lyrics, and his insistence on remaining a unique and removed character throughout everything. Many of the stars assembled at the Garden were faces from deep within Dylan's past: Eric Clapton, who had been inspired by *The Basement Tapes,* Tom Petty, with whom Dylan had toured, Kris Kristofferson, who had heard Dylan record *Blonde on Blonde* in 1966 while working at the Nashville studio as a janitor, and George Harrison, who, just before shaking up American music with the Beatles, had recognized Dylan's gifts as far back as 1964.

But the Madison Square Garden event, if it marked an anniversary, was not an ending. Confounding critics who thought that there was nothing Dylan could do that would surprise them anymore, he released *Good as I Been to You,* late in 1992, and *World Gone Wrong,* in the fall of 1993. On neither album did he play his own material, nor did he cover other popular hits. Instead, he went back to folk traditions such as the blues and did his own versions of older songs. Both albums revealed how worn

Dylan's voice had come to sound, but the expressiveness and fervor that he had always achieved through the simplicity of voice and guitar transcended age and situation. He reminded the world once again that the soul of a poet never diminishes but only travels and continues to speak. Some people might characterize his later albums as being rather dark or bleak. One can only speculate about the reason for the tone of these albums; Heylin wrote, "The only thing predictable about Dylan is that he will be unpredictable."

Surprising almost everyone, Dylan performed at the 25th anniversary of the Woodstock Music and Art Fair, held in Saugerties, New York. As the closing act on Sunday evening, August 14, 1994, Dylan opened with "Jokerman" and gave one of his vintage performances, backed by a four-piece band. He played many of his masterpieces, including "All Along the Watchtower"; "Highway 61 Revisited"; "It Takes a Lot to Laugh, It Takes a Train to Cry"; "Don't Think Twice, It's All Right"; "It Ain't Me, Babe"; "Rainy Day Women #12 & 35"; "Masters of War"; and "It's All Over Now, Baby Blue."

In 1985, Dylan reflected on his own contribution to the world of music:

> I was never going to be anything else. Never. All I wanted to do was play my guitar. It was a way of gaining attention, and whatever. It starts out that way . . . but I didn't know where it was going to lead. Now that it's led me here I still don't know where it is.

Dylan might not know where he has arrived, but perhaps that is because he has never stood still. He continues to move ahead, recording, performing, and exploring. He has taken his public through a lifetime filled with dramatic twists, surprises that show no signs of abating. He tours relentlessly, giving uneven performances and

As the sun sets on Sunday evening, August 14, 1994, Dylan's image is projected on a giant television screen during his closing performance at the 25th anniversary of the Woodstock Music and Art Fair in Saugerties, New York. He and his four-man backup band opened their act with "Jokerman."

playing in large arenas and in unexpected, low-profile places. His albums still defy the expectations of critics and fans alike, making it very apparent that Dylan and Dylan alone determines the path that he takes. The formidable pace that he sustains is more than simply dedicated; at times it seems almost frantic. Some speculate that he is running away from something in himself; others guess that performing live is all Dylan really wants to do now. But no one has been able to get through the distance that Dylan has put between himself and the public, so it has never been clear why he continues to make the choices he does. He remains elusive to a public that has never really been able to define him. In Shelton's biography of Dylan, one of Dylan's Woodstock friends says, "There's so many sides to Dylan, he's round." Dylan himself said in 1966, "It's lonely where I am," and perhaps performing onstage is the only way he can feel a little less alone.

Yet his role in rock history can be defined. Even before the Beatles, the Rolling Stones, and the Beach Boys, Dylan's ragged voice and searing pathos shaped the path of American music. His music and his poetry opened up the expressive possibilities of rock for his own and later generations. Phrases and images from his lyrics made their way into people's everyday language, and his brusque, unique voice became both a joking reference and a driving force for singer-songwriters. The association of rock music with social and political concerns took its very definition from Dylan. But he did not so much spearhead or define movements as coincide with them, while intent on his instinctive questions and ideas he followed his own path. Through his music and his actions, Dylan continues to speak not only to the feelings that are part of a life well explored, but to the understanding that it is only through a merciless and awkward struggle for honesty that one can truly experience that life.

A statement Dylan made in 1990 might best describe his view of that struggle:

> There's no one to my knowledge that isn't surprised by [his or her] longevity, including myself. But it's very dangerous to plan [far ahead], because you are dealing with your vanity. Tomorrow is hard enough. It's God who gives you the freedom, and the days you should be most concerned with are today and tomorrow.

Further Reading ★ ★ ★ ★ ★ ★ ★ ★ ★ ★ ★ ★ ★ ★ ★

Dylan, Bob. *Lyrics 1962–1985.* New York: Knopf, 1985.

———. *Tarantula.* 1971. Reprint. New York: Penguin Books, 1977.

Gray, Michael. *The Art of Bob Dylan: Song and Dance Man.* New York: St. Martin's, 1981.

Hampton, Wayne. *Guerrilla Minstrels.* Knoxville: University of Tennessee Press, 1986.

Helm, Levon, with Stephen Davis. *This Wheel's on Fire: The Story of the Band.* New York: Morrow, 1993.

Heylin, Clinton. *Bob Dylan: Behind the Shades.* New York: Summit Books, 1991.

Hoskyns, Barney. *Across the Great Divide: The Band and America.* New York: Hyperion, 1993.

Humphries, Patrick, and John Bauldie. *Absolutely Dylan: An Illustrated Biography.* New York: Viking Studio Books, 1991.

Scaduto, Anthony. *Bob Dylan: An Intimate Biography.* 1971. Rev. ed. New York: Signet/New American Library, 1979.

Shelton, Robert. *No Direction Home: The Life and Music of Bob Dylan.* New York: William Morrow, 1986.

Sloman, Larry. *On the Road with Bob Dylan: Rolling with the Thunder.* New York: Bantam Books, 1978.

Williams, Paul. *Bob Dylan, Performing Artist: The Early Years 1960–1973.* Novato, CA: Underwood-Miller, 1990.

Chronology ★

1941   Born Robert Allen Zimmerman on May 24 in Duluth, Minnesota

1959   Graduates form Hibbing High School and leaves home
for the University of Minnesota in Minneapolis

1961   Moves to New York City's Greenwich Village in January; critic Robert Shelton of
the *New York Times* writes a favorable review of Dylan's performance at Gerde's Folk
City in September; meets John Hammond of Columbia Records and signs a
recording contract in October; meets Suze Rotolo

1962   Dylan's first album, *Bob Dylan,* is released in March; he legally changes his name to
Bob Dylan in August; in mid-December, he travels to England for the first time

1963   Releases *Freewheelin' Bob Dylan* in May; begins association with Joan Baez and
performs with her at the Newport Folk Festival in July; sings at the civil rights March
on Washington on August 28

1964   Releases *The Times They Are A-Changin'* in February; visits Great Britain in May;
performs at the Newport Folk Festival in July; *Another Side of Bob Dylan* appears in
August

1965   Releases *Bringin' It All Back Home* in March; tours Great Britain in early spring, and
filmmaker D. A. Pennebaker documents the trip in the film *Don't Look Back*; Dylan
appears with the Paul Butterfield Blues Band at the Newport Folk Festival in July;
releases *Highway 61 Revisited* in August; meets the Hawks (later renamed the Band);
Marries Sara Lowndes on November 22

1966   Releases *Blonde on Blonde* in May; has motorcycle accident in Woodstock, New
York, on July 29

1967   Records with the Band at Big Pink from June to October

1968   Releases *John Wesley Harding* in January; performs at the Woody Guthrie Memorial
Concert at New York's Carnegie Hall on January 20

1969   *Nashville Skyline* is released in April; Woodstock Music and Art Fair, which Dylan
does not attend, takes place in Bethel on the weekend of August 15–17; Dylan
decides to perform with the Band at the Isle of Wight Festival in Great Britain
on August 31

1971   Dylan's novel, *Tarantula,* is published by Macmillan

1972   Dylan begins acting role as Alias in Sam Peckinpah's movie *Pat Garrett & Billy the
Kid* in November

1973   Dylan's book *Writings and Drawings* is published in June; after Dylan signs with
David Geffen's Asylum Records, Columbia retaliates with the release of *Dylan* in
November

1974 Asylum Records releases *Planet Waves* in January; Dylan takes art lessons from Norman Raeben in March; *Before the Flood* is released by Asylum in June; Dylan rejoins Columbia

1975 *Blood on the Tracks* is released in January; the *Basement Tapes,* songs originally recorded at Big Pink in 1967, is released in June; around November, Dylan puts together the Rolling Thunder Revue, and the group of musicians tour through the spring of 1976

1976 *Desire* is released in January; Dylan begins editing the film *Renaldo and Clara*

1977 Divorce from Sara is official in November

1978 *Renaldo and Clara,* originally four hours long, is finally released in January; in March, *Masterpieces* is released, followed by *Street-Legal* in June; Dylan picks up a crucifix thrown onto the stage at a concert in November and soon begins his involvement with the Vineyard Church and School of Discipleship

1979 *Slow Train Coming* is released in August

1980 In February, Dylan wins a Grammy Award for Best Male Rock Vocal Performance for "Gotta Serve Somebody"; *Saved* is released in June

1981 *Shot of Love* is released in August

1983 Dylan releases *Infidels* in November

1985 *Empire Burlesque* is released in June; Dylan performs at Live Aid in Philadelphia, Pennsylvania, in July; in September, he sings at the Farm Aid concert; five-album set *Biograph* is released in November; *Lyrics: 1962–1985* is published in December

1988 Releases *Down in the Groove* and joins friends George Harrison, Roy Orbison, Tom Petty, and Jeff Lynne as the Traveling Wilburys

1990 *Under the Red Sky* is released; records volume two with the Traveling Wilburys

1991 *The Bootleg Series* is released; in May, actor Jack Nicholson presents Dylan with the Lifetime Achievement Award at the Grammy Awards ceremony at New York's Radio City Music Hall

1992 Dylan's 30th anniversary celebration is held at New York's Madison Square Garden on October 16; album *Good as I Been to You* is released

1993 Album *World Gone Wrong* is released

1994 Dylan performs on August 14 with a four-piece backup band in Saugerties, New York, at the 25th anniversary of the Woodstock Music and Art Fair

Index ★

Susan Richardson is a curatorial staff member at the Rock and Roll Hall of Fame and Museum, a teacher, and a writer who lives in New York City. She holds an M.M. and a Ph.D. in musicology from Indiana University and has contributed to the *New Harvard Biographical Dictionary of Musicians*. She has written on both classical and popular music for the *Newsletter of the Institute for Studies in American Music* and *Rolling Stone*.

Leeza Gibbons is a reporter for and cohost of the nationally syndicated television program "Entertainment Tonight" and NBC's daily talk show "Leeza." A graduate of the University of South Carolina's School of Journalism, Gibbons joined the on-air staff of "Entertainment Tonight" in 1984 after cohosting WCBS-TV's "Two on the Town" in New York City. Prior to that, she cohosted "PM Magazine" on WFAA-TV in Dallas, Texas, and on KFDM-TV in Beaumont, Texas. Gibbons also hosts the annual "Miss Universe," "Miss U.S.A.," and "Miss Teen U.S.A." pageants, as well as the annual Hollywood Christmas Parade. She is active in a number of charities and has served as the national chairperson for the Spinal Muscular Atrophy Division of the Muscular Dystrophy Association; each September, Gibbons cohosts the National MDA Telethon with Jerry Lewis.